THE AMERICAN BAR ASSOCIATION LEGAL GUIDE FOR DOG OWNERS

Yolanda Eisenstein

ABA

Cover design by Amanda Fry/ABA Publishing.

Printed in the United States of America.

18 17 16 15 14 5 4 3 2 1

ISBN: 978-1-62722-915-9

e-ISBN: 978-1-62722-916-6

Library of Congress Cataloging-in-Publication Data

Eisenstein, Yolanda, author.
The American Bar Association legal guide for dog owners / Yolanda Eisenstein.
pages cm
Includes index.
ISBN 978-1-62722-915-9 (softcover : alk. paper)—ISBN 978-1-62722-916-6 (e-book) 1. Dogs—Law and legislation—United States 2. Dog owners—Legal status, laws, etc.—United States. I. Title.
KF390.5.D6E55 2014
346.7304'7—dc23 2014042716

Discounts are available for books ordered in bulk. Special consideration is given to state bars, CLE programs, and other bar-related organizations. Inquire at Book Publishing, ABA Publishing, American Bar Association, 321 N. Clark Street, Chicago, Illinois 60654-7598.

For the Dogs

Contents

About the Author

Yolanda Eisenstein is an animal lawyer in Dallas, Texas. She is an adjunct professor of animal law at Dedman School of Law at Southern Methodist University, vice chair of the American Bar Association Tort Trial and Insurance Practice Section Animal Law Committee, and an American Bar Foundation Fellow. She has served as chair of the American Bar Association TIPS Animal Law Committee and as chair of the State Bar of Texas Animal Law Section. Eisenstein is the author of the book *Careers in Animal Law*, and she is a contributor to *Animal Cruelty: A Multidisciplinary Approach to Understanding*. She has authored numerous articles and speaks regularly on animal law and animal protection issues.

Eisenstein graduated with honors from SMU Dedman School of Law and is licensed to practice law in Texas and New Mexico.

Acknowledgments

The fact that there is an audience for this book says much about the changing status of our companion animals and the many lawyers, advocates, and volunteers who have worked tirelessly to advance the cause of animals through the legal system. Through litigation, legislation, and an ongoing public policy debate, we have improved and saved the lives of many dogs. Thank you to everyone who has contributed to the achievements that are making life better for our companion animals.

Thank you to Don Feare, Barbara Gislason, Debra Hamilton, Susan Hightower, Linda Solomon, Claire Schwarz, Randy Turner, and Robert Udashen for their advice and counsel on the book. A special thank you to Julie Fershtman, who contributed the section on pet insurance in chapter 3.

As always, thank you to my family. To my parents, who, to this day, cannot turn away a sick or hungry animal who wanders into their yard. To Skylar, my four-legged furry girl, who spends her days lying next to me while waiting for walks and romps in the park. And to Abram, for happily marrying me, and my dog.

Introduction

This is a book about dogs and the law. More specifically, it is a book about knowing and understanding the law and how to protect yourself and your dog. It is also a tool and a guide to using the law to advocate for the well-being of all animals.

Dogs are everywhere, and what amazing creatures they are. They come in all shapes and sizes, matched only by their many purposes and contributions to our lives. Dogs are faithful companions and dedicated workers. They comfort child victims who have to testify in court, and they are the eyes of those who cannot see. Military dogs sniff out bombs, saving the lives of soldiers, and simply petting a dog has been shown to lower blood pressure. Dogs are truly amazing.

It is difficult to imagine that in the United States in recent history, dogs were so low in status that they did not even warrant a legal classification. Livestock, such as cows and pigs, were valuable property while dogs remained on the sidelines. Today, dogs are classified as property, along with all animals, and they remain so in the legal sense but not in the minds and hearts of most dog owners. Research repeatedly shows that for most of us, our dogs are like family members, and in some cases they are even equal in status to children. Society has come a long way.

About the Book

I am an animal protection lawyer. I have written this book for anyone interested in how the law treats dogs, not only within the context of their role as companions but in everything from pet trusts to dog fighting. Everyone will find valuable insights into how the law treats dogs. A lawyer who is not familiar with animal law will find it helpful when a family law or estate client walks into her office with a dog issue, which is happening with increasing frequency.

This book covers the many laws that affect dogs. From a city's leash ordinance to a federal ban on products that contain dog fur, the laws are expansive and are found at every level of government. Because of the extent of the laws and the fact that they vary by state, it is impossible to cover every dog law in detail. For those that are state driven, I have provided a law or a court case from a specific state as an example. You will find Texas mentioned often, given that it is the state where I practice. However, the Internet has made it easy to find laws, and you should have no trouble finding your state's law on any given subject.

I recommend reading the book from beginning to end on the first reading. The first few chapters cover the status of dogs as property and set out the basics of the law and where to find it. These are important sections in that they lay the foundation for the remainder of the book.

Terminology

The vocabulary we use to describe our pets, who are now referred to as companion animals, is changing. There is a movement to use the word "guardian" rather than "owner" to more accurately depict our relationship with our dogs. While this new language is a positive step in describing the status of our four-legged companions, the law has yet to fully incorporate these terms. Therefore, I have stayed with words such as "owner" and "pet" when they are consistent with the law.

One concession I have not made is in referring to a dog as an "it." Until and unless we find a better term, I find it impossible to refer to our living, breathing companions as "things" and prefer to use the term "who." In gender references, I have alternately used the pronouns "he" and "she" throughout the book.

I use various legal terms, which I define. The appendix contains a list of those terms and their definitions.

Special Features

Two unique features can be found throughout the book. For lawyers who are not familiar with animal law and want to know more, there are specific segments labeled "For Lawyers" in which I have offered suggestions or shared an experience that may be helpful. Likewise, for everyone reading the book, I have done the same in segments called "For Everyone."

Finally, further insights, specific laws, and court cases are presented in sections called "Case in Point." While optional, these readings add detail and perspective to the laws and information presented.

Enough said. Read on to enhance your legal knowledge about dogs and the law.

Chapter 1

DOGS AS PROPERTY

Dogs are classified as property within the United States legal system. While it seems relatively simple and straightforward, the classification of dogs, and of all animals, as property is probably the most important, as well as the most controversial, concept in animal law. It is important in that all laws related to dogs are built upon, and have evolved from, animals' status as property. It is controversial because society's changing views of animals have posed inherent moral and ethical issues that surround classifying a living, sentient being as property. If you have not given much thought to the fact that your dog is property, it is time to consider it. Understanding the implications, legal and otherwise, of your dog's status as property will assist you in making informed decisions, knowing your rights, and protecting your dog.

What Is Property?

What exactly is "property" under the law? Most of us view property in the traditional sense, as something tangible that we own, such as cars, furniture, and computers. These types of items are considered personal property, and our dogs are included in that category. Another type of property is real property, which is the land that you own and the home and any other structures on the land. And a third type of property is intellectual property, creative ideas that can be granted exclusive legal rights, such as patents. These ideas may be in tangible form, such as mechanical devices, or they may be formulas or concepts that are new and novel. And if you are wondering whether dogs can be patented, the answer is yes. The Patent and Trademark Office (PTO) has granted more than 800 patents on live animals, including dogs.[1] As you might imagine, these types of patents are not without controversy and have been challenged by animal advocates and watchdog organizations.

Case in Point

In 1999, the University of Texas compromised the immune system of 31 beagles in order to mimic humans with weakened immune systems. The dogs received daily doses of steroids and were exposed to various levels of radiation, and then the weakened beagles were infected with mold. In 2002, the experimenter obtained a patent for the impaired beagle model. The American Anti-Vivisection Society and the PatentWatch Project of the International Center for Technology Assessment filed a challenge to the patent. The PTO agreed to reexamine the patent, although the public outcry in opposition resulted in the university disclaiming the patent in 2004.[2]

In law, property is not a simple or one-dimensional concept. Beyond its various forms and tangible attributes is the idea of the legal rights we have in the property we own. Our car or computer can be defined as an "external thing over which the rights of possession, use, and enjoyment are exercised."[3] Any lawyer who is reading this book will remember the "bundle of rights" lessons from property law. When applied to our dogs, inevitable

1. Tracie Letterman, Crystal Miller-Spiegel & Nina Mak, *Patently Cruel: Animals Are Not Inventions*, THE BRIEF (Summer 2011), http://www.americanbar.org/publications/the_brief/2010_11/summer_2011.html.
2. *Id.*
3. BLACK'S LAW DICTIONARY 1232 (7th ed. 1999) (emphasis added).

disagreements arise regarding what "uses" are acceptable or what constitutes the "enjoyment" of our dogs. So it is easy to see how the rights in our dogs as property can be the source of legal conflicts and personal debates.

A Brief History

How did dogs become property? In order to answer that question, we need to take a step back and look at the development of all animals as property. In the 19th and early 20th centuries, our country was still largely agricultural. We used animals for food, clothing, and transportation. Even in cities, horses pulled carts and provided transportation. Many of our critical possessions and financial assets were tied up in land and animals—sheep, cows, horses, and pigs. Dogs were not included in those assets, as they had no ascertainable value at the time. Of course people had dogs and loved them as we do, but the law had yet to recognize them. It was important that people had title, legally recognized rights of possession and ownership, to their livestock. Legal title gave them the ability to buy and sell animals and gave them rights to the animals' offspring. And while not always the case, the obligation to feed and protect those animals was usually assured since the owners were the ones who benefited from healthy, productive animals.

Eventually dogs and other domesticated animals were added to the category of property and that is where they remain today. As property, dogs and other animals can be owned and sold by individuals, private corporations, or organizations. In contrast, wild animals roaming freely on public lands, such as deer, fowl, and rabbits, are owned and managed by state and federal governments. Part of that management responsibility includes conservation and protection of the animals while at the same time allowing individuals to safely enjoy public lands through hiking, camping, and boating. Unless a species is endangered, hunting, trapping, and fishing laws allow people to take, and own, wild animals during certain times and under certain conditions.

Should Dogs Be Property?

We have come a long way since the 19th and early 20th centuries. We are no longer predominately an agricultural society but the legal status of dogs as property is still with us today. Some of you may be thinking, "OK, dogs are property; what's the problem?" And for many dog owners, there is no problem. The law is established in our legal system and seems to work well, so what's the fuss? For others, however, it is difficult to think of a dog as property, as a "thing" with no legal rights and with the monetary value of a chair. How can a living, sentient being who sleeps in your bed and licks your face be a thing?

The reality is that your dog is clearly not a thing and in many ways this example is a simple one for a complex issue that has no easy answer. Whether dogs should be property is largely a matter of a personal opinion, and more importantly it is a legal and public policy issue that is currently being debated and played out throughout the country.

Case in Point

There is a movement to change the property status of animals by changing the status of humans from dog "owners" to dog "guardians," a term that many believe is a more appropriate description of our relationship with dogs. This line of reasoning mirrors that of family law, where children or individuals who have disabilities that prevent them from fully caring for themselves have guardians appointed by the court. These guardians do not "own" their wards, as we own our dogs, but they care for them and make decisions for them while allowing those in their care to be as independent as possible.

This movement to change our relationship with our companion animals has taken hold in a few jurisdictions. For example, in 2000, Boulder, Colorado, changed its city code to include "guardian" when referring to a companion animal's "owner."[4] The following year, Rhode Island added the word "guardian" to its definitions related to animals. However, the extent to which the designation meaningfully changes the legal relationship we have with our dogs is negligible, as the term "guardian" means "a person(s) having the

4. R. Scott Nolen, *Owners or Guardians? Cities Change Identity of Pet Owners, Hoping to Promote Welfare*, J. AM. VETERINARY MED. ASS'N NEWS (Apr. 15, 2001), http://www.avma.org/onlnews/javma/apr01/s041501b.asp. *See also* BOULDER MUNICIPAL CODE § 6-1-2 (2005).

same rights and responsibilities of an owner, and both terms shall be used interchangeably."[5] It is clear from the language and history of Rhode Island's bill that the legislature did not intend to make "guardian" totally distinct from "owner"; however, it was a progressive step in increasing awareness, and it was a public expression of a shift in attitude.[6] What these laws reveal, and what lawyers in particular should notice, is the progressive nature of the people who pass these laws. Their views will be reflected in the elected city officials, judges, and lawmakers who have chosen to make a statement about animal protection.

The debate regarding dogs as property is an important one, but it is well beyond the scope of this book. Many excellent books and articles address the subject, and I encourage you to read them. What you need to know, as a dog owner, lawyer, or advocate, are the basics and how your dog's status as property affects you and your dog. Your dog's economic value, your ownership rights, and your obligations are tied to property concepts. The extent to which you are affected is determined by each state, and there are as many different laws, court cases, and ordinances as there are breeds of dogs. Some laws place a limit on the value of a dog in the event of wrongful death, and some leave it to the courts. Some states allow emotional distress damages for the loss of a dog, and some do not.

The only certainty in animal law is that there is no certainty or consistency. There are always exceptions and gray areas in which dogs are not treated as property or in which they are treated as a special type of property. The most obvious examples are the animal cruelty laws that make it a crime for you, or anyone else, to harm your dog under certain circumstances. You are generally free to do whatever you wish with your other property, such as tossing your old television set in the dumpster, but you cannot toss your dog in the dumpster.

Also, in most states today, your dog can be the beneficiary of a pet trust, a legally binding trust, that allows you to leave money specifically for the care of your dog in the event of your death or disability. While your dog's designated caregiver actually receives the funds, she is bound by law to

5. R.I. GEN. LAWS § 4-1-1 (2013).
6. *Id.*

use those funds to care for your dog, and not for any other purpose. Your television set cannot be the beneficiary of a trust.

So if dogs should not be considered property or persons, what should they be? Perhaps they are special property or "living property."[7] Keep these thoughts in mind as you read on to learn more about how dogs are treated under the law and as you make your own decision about dogs as property, persons, or children.

7. David Favre, *In Living Property: A New Status for Animals within the Legal System*, 93 MARQ. L. Rev. 1021 (2010), *available at* http://scholarship.law.marquette.edu/mulr/vol93/iss3/3. David Favre, professor of law and the Nancy Heathcote Professor of Property and Animal Law at Michigan State University College of Law, has proposed an additional category of property for animals known as living property. He explains why animals should receive consideration in the legal system and what some of those legal rights might be.

Chapter 2

THE DOG LAWS

The laws related to dogs are found primarily at the state and local levels. Each city and state has individual needs and the authority to address those needs through legislation. State legislatures pass wide-ranging laws that apply to residents throughout the state, and cities enact local ordinances that serve their specific needs. For example, dangerous-dog laws are important health and safety issues for all residents and are enacted at the statewide level. However, barking dogs may constitute a nuisance in a city apartment but not in a rural town where your closest neighbor is a mile away. And, the laws will vary throughout the United States, with each state having its own individual needs based on the economics, politics, and policies of that state. Situations in Texas, with vast expanses of land and agriculture, will be very different from the issues faced in Rhode Island, where there are miles of waterfront. This diversity in character among the states means diversity among the laws. It unfortunately creates a patchwork of laws, resulting in some states having stringent animal protection laws and others having little protection.[1]

1. Humane Society of the United States State Rankings 2013, http://www.humanesociety.org/about/state/humane-state-ranking-2013.html?credit=web_id154209008 (last visited Sept. 5, 2014).

Dog laws are also found at the federal level and govern large-scale and cross-border activities, such as commercial puppy sales, the transportation of animals, and serious crimes such as organized dog fighting and crush videos. These laws also address the use of animals in research, trade in animal products, and the use of service dogs under the Americans with Disabilities Act.

Finally, the U.S. Constitution is the guiding law of the land that establishes our rights as U.S. citizens and protects us from unjustified intrusions by the government.

Statutory (Written) Laws

Statutory laws are written laws, the result of the work of Congress, state legislatures, and city councils. Lawmaking is no easy task, as senators and representatives fight to pass laws that benefit their constituents, sometimes to the detriment of others. These fights take place in Washington, D.C., and in every state. Despite the fights and the gridlock, lawmakers manage to set aside their differences on some issues and pass laws, including laws about dogs.

Rules and Regulations

The legislative process does not end with passing laws. Laws are often written as broad mandates that may leave out more than they include. After laws are passed, various rules, regulations, and orders are developed and implemented to interpret and give meaning to the laws. These "regs," as they are often called, are administered by various agencies at state and federal levels.

Case in Point

Texas passed a "puppy mill" law, the Texas Dog or Cat Breeders Act, to regulate the sales of puppies in an effort to stop the cruelty associated with puppy mills.[2] The Texas Department of Licensing and Regulation is the agency that has developed the rules and regulations and is charged with administering the law. The rule-making process was extensive and open to public comment, as is federal rule-making as well.

At the national level of government, the Animal and Plant Health Inspection Service (APHIS) is an agency of the U.S. Department of Agriculture (USDA) that is responsible for, among other activities, the administration of the Animal Welfare Act. It explains its role as follows:

> The Animal and Plant Health Inspection Service is a multi-faceted Agency with a broad mission area that includes protecting and promoting US agricultural health, regulating genetically engineered organisms, **administering the Animal Welfare Act** and carrying out wildlife damage management activities. These efforts support the overall mission of USDA, which is to protect and promote food, agriculture, natural resources and related issues.[3]

There is a distinct area of the law, termed administrative law, that deals exclusively with rules and regulatory agencies. Lawyers in the field of administrative law spend time studying rules and regulations and subsequent changes in order to stay abreast of any rules that may affect their clients and their businesses.

The Common Law

Up to this point, the discussion has focused on statutory, or written, laws. Our system of law in the United States is referred to as the common law, a

---

2. Puppy mills are large-scale commercial breeding operations that place profit ahead of the welfare of the dogs, often resulting in inhumane conditions. *See* chapter 4, "When Problems Arise."

3. USDA ANIMAL & PLANT HEALTH INSPECTION SERVICE, http://www.aphis.usda.gov/about_aphis/ (last visited Sept. 6, 2014) (emphasis added).

body of law consisting of judicial decisions that have been handed down through the years. These decisions are the legal precedent for similar cases that follow. Everyone has heard of the common law. This legal system has been with us since our early days as a country and is based on the common law of England. It is established in every state except Louisiana, whose law is based on the French civil code.

The common law is developed in two ways: (1) through judicial decisions in court cases, and (2) through a court's interpretation of statutory laws. In judicial decisions, judges decide court cases based on the rulings of previous similar court cases, either maintaining or creating new legal precedent. In the interpretation of statutory laws, judges construe the meaning of a statute where there may be questions or ambiguity related to the written law at issue. A judge may interpret a statute's meaning through its language or legislative intent; determine who is affected by it; or rule on its constitutionality.

So, in looking at the big legal picture, we have the U.S. Constitution, which establishes our rights as U.S. citizens; federal laws that address cross-border activities and concerns at the national and international levels; the laws of the 50 states that govern the residents of the individual states; and local laws, or ordinances, that apply specifically to a particular city or town. Federal and state agencies administer rules, regulations, and policies that clarify, implement, and support the laws. And the common law is the system that ties it all together.

As U.S. citizens, whether we think about it or not, we play a significant role in the passage, enforcement, and administration of all of these laws. Through voting, public comment, filing lawsuits, and caring about our canines, we contribute to public policy and influence how our legal system governs our treatment of animals.

Civil Law and Criminal Law

Our legal system is comprised of two broad categories of law—civil and criminal. The most obvious example of a criminal dog law is a felony law against animal cruelty. Minor crimes are known as misdemeanors and can include negligent acts of cruelty or nuisance violations, such as barking dogs.

Criminal lawsuits are brought by the government and are considered crimes against society. They are punished with fines and/or jail time.

Civil law deals with disputes between individuals, organizations, or companies and involves monetary compensation to the party found to have been wronged. Private parties pursue civil cases, although the government can be a party. An example of a civil case related to dogs would be a lawsuit against a dog owner by a person who has been bitten. The table below distinguishes some of the differences between civil and criminal law.

	Civil Law	Criminal Law
Definition	Disputes between private parties	Crimes against the country, state, or municipality
Parties	Private	Government
Purpose	To award compensation when one party has injured another party	To correct a wrong against society and punish the perpetrator
Investigation	Each party is responsible for gathering and presenting evidence	The government investigates and must build its case against the person charged with a crime
Heard	Judge or Judge and Jury	Judge or Judge and Jury
Punishment	Monetary damages, or sometimes specific performance of a job	Fines and/or jail time as well as other punishments allowed under the law
Examples	Wrongful death or injury to a person's companion animal	Felony animal cruelty

The Supreme Law of the Land

The U.S. Constitution is known as the supreme law of the land, meaning that no other laws come before the Constitution. With most dog laws found at the local and state levels, you may be wondering where the Constitution fits in. This is where our dog's current classification as property is key. Unlike the state and local laws that inform us of our legal obligations regarding the treatment of our dogs, the Constitution grants us certain rights regarding our dogs, and protection of them, based on their property status. These rights may be violated if the government unreasonably interferes with our ownership of our dog or seizes her without due process.

The First Amendment

In addition to our constitutional right to possess and own property, including dogs, we also have the right to speak publicly and freely, within certain constraints, about everything from puppy mills to dog parks.

> Congress shall make no law respecting an establishment of religion, or prohibiting the free exercise thereof; or abridging the freedom of speech, or of the press; or the right of the people peaceably to assemble, and to petition the Government for a redress of grievances.[4]

The First Amendment rights to speech and to petition our government are fundamental and vital to animal advocates who choose to publicly voice their opinions regarding the treatment of animals, whether in circuses, scientific research, or puppy mills. Through the First Amendment, advocates give voice to the animals who cannot speak for themselves.

The right to free speech is not absolute. Cities are allowed to regulate certain aspects of speech, such as prohibiting bullhorns and keeping streets passable and safe. Most of us know you cannot yell "Fire!" in a movie theater if there is no fire. However, the right to speak freely is fundamental, and cities must have very good reasons for any restraints they place on public protests.

Additionally, the establishment and free exercise clauses, the two religious clauses of the First Amendment, are relevant to animals used in religions, such as the Santeria, who sacrifice animals as part of their liturgy. In the most prominent case regarding animal sacrifice, *Church of Lukumi Babalu Aye v. City of Hialeah*, the U.S. Supreme Court struck down the city of Hialeah's ordinances that had banned the practice and upheld the Santeria's right to sacrifice animals as part of their religion. The court stated that a "law burdening religious practice that is not neutral or not of general application must undergo the most rigorous scrutiny."[5] Hialeah's ordinances did not survive that scrutiny, and while the Santeria do not sacrifice dogs, a religion that does sacrifice dogs would be analyzed under the Supreme Court's ruling in this case.

---

4. U.S. CONST. amend. I.
5. Church of Lukumi Babalu Aye v. City of Hialeah, 508 U.S. 520, 546 (1993).

Chilling Free Speech

Recently, citizens who have spoken publicly against the acts of corporations and individuals have found themselves the victims of lawsuits known as strategic lawsuits against public participation (SLAPPs). SLAPPs are a form of intimidation that some corporations and individuals are using to silence their critics by forcing them to spend money to defend lawsuits against them that are usually baseless. These lawsuits can be effective even without merit because those being sued may be forced to spend thousands of dollars in attorney's fees and related costs to defend themselves. Victims of these suits may have to apologize or claim they have made misstatements, even if that is against their beliefs, in order to save themselves from financial ruin defending a baseless suit against a plaintiff with money.

Fortunately, states are acting to protect our First Amendment rights by passing anti-SLAPP laws to stop baseless suits and to punish those who bring them. California is one example.

Case in Point

California Anti-SLAPP Motion

> (a) The Legislature finds and declares that there has been a disturbing increase in lawsuits brought primarily to chill the valid exercise of the constitutional rights of freedom of speech and petition for the redress of grievances. The Legislature finds and declares that it is in the public interest to encourage continued participation in matters of public significance, and that this participation should not be chilled through abuse of the judicial process. . . .
> (b)(1) A cause of action against a person arising from any act of that person in furtherance of the person's right of petition or free speech under the United States Constitution or the California Constitution in connection with a public issue shall be subject to a special motion to strike, unless the court determines that the plaintiff has established that there is a probability that the plaintiff will prevail on the claim. . . .
> (e) As used in this section, "act in furtherance of a person's right of

Continued

Case in Point *Continued*

petition or free speech under the United States or California Constitution in connection with a public issue" includes: . . . (3) any written or oral statement or writing made in a place open to the public or a public forum in connection with an issue of public interest, or (4) any other conduct in furtherance of the exercise of the constitutional right of petition or the constitutional right of free speech in connection with a public issue or an issue of public interest.[6]

The Fourth Amendment

The Fourth Amendment guards against unreasonable searches of our homes and seizures of our possessions, including our dogs.

> The right of the people to be secure in their persons, houses, papers, and effects, against unreasonable searches and seizures, shall not be violated, and no Warrants shall issue, but upon probable cause, supported by Oath or affirmation, and particularly describing the place to be searched, and the persons or things to be seized.[7]

A seizure occurs when there has been a significant interference with a person's interest in property that can be physically seized. The confiscation of dogs that are deemed to be dangerous and police shootings of dogs are two of the most common examples of seizures that may give rise to constitutional challenges under the Fourth Amendment.

The Fourteenth Amendment

The Fourteenth Amendment contains the due process clause as it is applied to the individual states.[8]

6. CAL. CIV. PROC. CODE § 425.16 (West 2011).
7. U.S. CONST. amend. IV.
8. The Fifth Amendment has a due process clause, but the Fourteenth Amendment due process clause applies to the states where dangerous-dog shootings and police shootings are normally heard.

> All persons born or naturalized in the United States, and subject to the jurisdiction thereof, are citizens of the United States and of the State wherein they reside. No State shall make or enforce any law which shall abridge the privileges or immunities of citizens of the United States; nor shall any State deprive any person of life, liberty, or property, without due process of law; nor deny to any person within its jurisdiction the equal protection of the laws.[9]

The right to due process requires that citizens must be afforded rights such as adequate notice and an opportunity to be heard when the state or federal government acts in a manner that deprives a citizen of life, liberty, or property. Due process violations by governments, such as the following example, may occur in dog seizure cases.

Case in Point

In the case of *Van Patten v. City of Binghamton*, hearing officer Stephen Jensen issued a decision that James Van Patten's dog Shadow was dangerous and was to be humanely euthanized.[10] The court found that the city, through its process and procedures that resulted in the euthanization of Shadow, deprived Van Patten of his right to seek judicial review.[11] In a violation of procedural due process, the city acted contrary to its statute, stated no reasons for the determination to euthanize the dog as due process would require, and deprived Van Patten of his right to appeal.[12]

Other Constitutional Claims

In addition to the constitutional claims just described, other claims may arise based on: vagueness, the doctrine that criminal laws must be explicit and specifically define what conduct is criminal; the denial of equal protection

9. U.S. CONST. amend. XIV, § 1.
10. Van Patten v. City of Binghamton, 137 F. Supp. 2d 98 (N.D.N.Y. 2001).
11. *Id.* at 104–05.
12. *Id.* at 105–06.

under the law; or prior restraint, a government act that prohibits speech or expression before it occurs.

FOR LAWYERS: Constitutional animal-related litigation is brought under the Civil Rights Act of 1871.[13] The law was originally passed to provide a civil remedy to freed African-American slaves who continued to be denied their constitutional rights by government officials. One of the ways Section 1983 is used today is to file constitutional claims for harm to animal owners.

FOR EVERYONE: Violations of our constitutional rights are serious. The law is complex and in most instances requires the assistance of an experienced lawyer, particularly in an animal-related case. If you believe your rights have been violated, contact a lawyer. There are nonprofit legal organizations that can advise you.

Federal Law

For most of us, federal laws do not have the same day-to-day impact on our lives as those at the state and local levels. While there are federal laws related to dogs, most of them address dealers who sell dogs for research, large-scale breeding operations, and dog fighting and other crimes. Although most dog owners do not need to be too concerned with federal oversight, anyone who cares about dogs should be informed about the law. It is always a good idea to know what the federal government is doing to protect our canine companions and us as U.S. citizens. If you are a lawyer who wants to be well versed in animal law, you will need to know the federal laws that cover dogs and all animals.

Federal laws regulate the commercial sale, transportation, and treatment of dogs; criminalize acts of animal cruelty, such as dog fighting and crush videos; regulate the treatment of service dogs under the Americans with Disabilities Act; direct the states to enact legislation on how pets are to be handled in the event of disasters; and require the licensing and regulation of dogs sold for scientific research as well as those sold to consumers as animal companions.

13. 42 U.S.C. § 1983 (2014).

The Animal Welfare Act

Dogs Used in Scientific Research

An important, albeit complex and comprehensive, federal law related to dogs is the Animal Welfare Act (AWA), which was first passed in 1966. It was enacted in response to a public outcry over the theft of dogs that were family dogs who were then sold to research laboratories. Labs use dogs, as well as rats, mice, birds, cats, primates, guinea pigs, and other animals, in scientific research. At the time of the AWA's passage, there were no laws, standards, or rules addressing where the dogs came from and whether or not they had owners. As a result, thieves were stealing family pets and selling them for research, with no negative consequences for the seller or the purchaser. The use of family dogs in research struck a nerve with the public and Congress responded with the AWA. In its original statement of policy, Congress maintained that regulation was necessary for the following reasons:

> (1) to insure that animals intended for use in research facilities or for exhibition purposes or for use as pets are provided humane care and treatment;
> (2) to assure the humane treatment of animals during transportation in commerce; and
> (3) to protect the owners of animals from the theft of their animals by preventing the sale or use of animals which have been stolen.[14]

Although Congress used the term "animal" in its policy statement, rats, mice, and birds are excluded from the definition of "animal" in the AWA.[15]

The AWA applies to animal dealers and exhibitors and covers many species of animals, including dogs. Since 1966, it has been amended numerous times in response to lawsuits and in an effort to bring it in line with current laws and practices. In its oversight of the treatment of dogs, the law regulates the activities of "dealers" who buy and sell dogs for use in research,

14. 7 U.S.C.A. § 2131 (2014).
15. The secretary of agriculture's 1972 regulations under the AWA excluded birds, mice, rats, horses, and farm animals from the definition of "animal." After various challenges over the years, the 2002 Farm Bill contained an amendment by Jesse Helms (R-NC) to exclude birds, mice, and rats bred for research from the AWA definition of "animal." President George W. Bush signed the bill into law.

teaching, and exhibition, and of those who sell dogs as pets. It defines a dealer as a person who "in commerce, for compensation or profit, delivers for transportation or transports, except as a carrier, buys, or sells, or negotiates the purchase or sale of any dog . . . whether alive or dead for research, teaching [veterinary schools], exhibition [dog shows], or use as a pet, or (2) any dog for hunting, security, or breeding purposes."[16] The law specifically exempts retail pet stores (brick-and-mortar stores), unless the store is selling dogs wholesale or for scientific research. It also exempts any person, generally referred to as a hobby breeder, who sells dogs but derives no more than $500 gross income in a calendar year from the sales; maintains a total of three or fewer breeding female dogs, and sells only the offspring, which were born and raised on the premises; or any person who sells fewer than 25 dogs per year for research, teaching, or testing or to any research facility and is not otherwise required to obtain a license.[17]

So if you are a dealer, how does it work? First, it means you are required to obtain a license in order to buy and sell dogs for research and the other purposes covered by the law. In order to obtain a license you must meet the standards promulgated by the secretary of agriculture. You must maintain detailed records of the purchase, sale, transportation, identification, and previous ownership of dogs; mark or identify each live dog (in a humane manner); observe a holding period of five days before selling a dog; and be subject to ongoing inspections to determine whether any violations exist.

On the purchaser side, research facilities, handlers, carriers, and unlicensed exhibitors must register with the secretary of agriculture.[18] They may purchase dogs only from licensed dealers or auction houses. Research facilities are required to observe humane standards under the rules and regulations for the handling, care, treatment, and transportation of dogs, including exercise for dogs and primates.[19] Standards include "handling, housing, feeding, watering, sanitation, ventilation, shelter from extremes of weather and temperatures, and adequate veterinary care."[20] The law also requires the use of anesthetic, analgesic, or tranquilizing drugs, when

16. 7 U.S.C.A. § 2132(f) (2013).
17. 7 U.S.C.A. § 2132(h)(2013).
18. 7 U.S.C.A. § 2137 (2013).
19. *Id.* § 2143 (2013).
20. *Id.* § 2143(a)(2)(A) (2013).

such use would be proper in the opinion of the attending veterinarian.[21] However, animals may be subjected to painful experimentation if deemed necessary by the researcher.[22]

The AWA is not without its detractors. The use of animals in scientific experiments is controversial, and animal advocates continue to push for the elimination of the use of animals in research. Most recently, the National Institutes of Health announced that it would "substantially reduce" the use of chimpanzees in NIH-funded biomedical research and designate for retirement most of the chimpanzees it currently owns or supports.[23]

Despite any controversy, the law's patchwork of rules and regulations and comprehensive nature make it difficult to enforce. Sufficient resources are not allotted for inspections, and the law lags behind advances in technology and society's changing attitudes. As a citizen it is difficult to challenge the law because it has no citizen suit provision, meaning that no provision in the law specifically allows a citizen to file a lawsuit. Plaintiffs must look to the Administrative Procedures Act, which can be used to bring the USDA under judicial review for enforcement of the AWA. Other laws have citizen suit provisions, providing a more direct path to challenge the law.

Case in Point

The Clean Water Act has a citizen suit provision:

> (a) Except as provided in subsection (b) of this section and section 309(g)(6), **any citizen may commence a civil action on his own behalf**—(1) against any person (including (i) the United States, and (ii) any other governmental instrumentality or agency to the extent permitted by the eleventh amendment to the constitution) who is alleged to be in violation of (A) an effluent standard or limitation under this Act or (b) an order issued by the Administrator or a State with respect to such a standard or limitation, or

Continued

21. *Id.* § 2143(a)(3) (2013).
22. *Id.* § 2143 (2013).
23. *NIH to Reduce Significantly the Use of Chimpanzees in Research*, NAT'L INST. HEALTH, http://www.nih.gov/news/health/jun2013/od-26.htm (last visited Sept. 6, 2014).

Case in Point *Continued*

(2) against the Administrator where there is alleged a failure of the Administrator to perform any act of duty under this Act which is not discretionary with the Administrator.[24]

The Internet and Pet Stores

The Internet has drastically changed many aspects of our lives, including the purchase of puppies. In the past, when we wanted a purebred dog, we found a breeder nearby, indicated our desire for a new dog, and waited for the breeder's dog to deliver a litter of puppies. Once the puppies were born, we visited the breeder, carefully scrutinized all of the puppies, and chose our favorite. We waited for him to grow old enough to be weaned from his mother's care, and we could then take him home. We met the breeder, our puppy's mom, and the siblings.

Unfortunately, today many people surf the Internet or go to a pet store where you can purchase a puppy and take her home or have her shipped to you immediately. The problem with that approach is that many of these dogs may come from puppy mills, some from as far away as Eastern Europe. The facilities are puppy factories, where there is inbreeding, little to no veterinary care, and no regulations or oversight. The breeding females live in inhumane conditions, and by purchasing a puppy in this manner, consumers contribute to the cruelty. The puppies may lack appropriate vaccinations or have genetic problems and diseases.

Case in Point

The California Assembly Office of Research found a 48-percent chance that the state's pet store puppies are ill or incubating an illness at the time of purchase.[25]

24. 33 U.S.C.A. § 1365 (2014) (emphasis added).
25. Cindy A. Adams, *Puppy Mills, The Tragedy Continues*, http://www.petfinder.com/helping-pets/puppy-mills/puppy-mills-tragedy-continues (last visited Sept. 6, 2014).

The law prohibits puppies from being shipped when they are younger than eight weeks old and weaned.[26] Many are actually shipped at a younger age, frightened and alone and away from the safety and care of their mothers, and some die in transit. Puppies who are separated prematurely from their mother and siblings may experience behavioral problems as adult dogs. As a buyer, you never see the puppy, the breeder, the facility, or the puppy's parents before you buy. While you have legal rights, those rights are often difficult and expensive to enforce when the breeder is in cyberspace. You may have only a website, a phone number, or an e-mail address, and the breeder could be in a foreign country. Your options are few when the breeder fails to answer your e-mails or phone calls.

The Internet was not a factor in the original passage of the AWA in 1966, and there are loopholes that allow some of the most egregious violators to skirt the law by claiming retail pet store exemptions. After increasing complaints from the public regarding the lack of oversight of dogs sold over the Internet and a report from the Office of Inspector General (OIG) audit recommendation, APHIS recently proposed a rule change to bring these Internet sellers under the auspices of the AWA. The OIG report found that 80 percent of sampled breeders were not licensed under the AWA because they sold pets over the Internet and claimed retail pet store status. Retail pet stores are currently exempt from the AWA, but the new rule tightens the definition of "retail pet store" to mean a place of business or residence at which the seller, buyer, and the animal available for sale are physically present. Internet sellers cannot meet this requirement unless they have a physical location as well as a website. This regulation allows buyers to personally observe the dog before purchasing him to determine whether or not the dog appears healthy. It is not foolproof, but it does provide a location and a way to contact the seller in the event of a problem. Internet sellers can no longer claim the retail pet store exemption, which makes them subject to inspections under the AWA.

Also, the AWA added a section in 2008 that regulates the importation of live dogs.[27] The law directs importers, any persons who import a dog from a foreign country for resale, to comply with various requirements. The dog is to be in good health, vaccinated, and at least six months old.[28]

26. 9 C.F.R. § 2.130.
27. 7 U.S.C.A. § 2148 (2013).
28. *Id.* § 2148(b)(1) (2013).

FOR EVERYONE: Hopefully, the obvious hazards and cruelty that may accompany the purchase of a dog over the Internet have convinced you to use the Internet as a research tool rather than as an end in itself. Do your due diligence on the entity you are considering. While there are reputable Internet sellers, the unknown looms large. If you find an Internet seller in your area, go visit the facility to make sure you are not contributing to a puppy mill operation.

Dog Fighting and the AWA

The crime of dog fighting is brutal, and laws are found at federal and state levels. The AWA makes it a crime to sponsor or exhibit an animal in a fighting venture; to buy, sell, possess, train, transport, deliver, or receive an animal for the purpose of fighting; and to use the U.S. Postal Service or any other interstate instrumentality to promote or further a fight.[29] Animal fighting mainly involves dogs and roosters (cockfighting), but the law includes any mammal or bird "except man."[30] The law also makes it a crime to buy, sell, deliver, or transport sharp instruments used in cockfighting.[31]

There are state laws that criminalize dog fighting, and they vary in their reach and levels of punishment. Concerned legislators continue to pass laws that bring those who fight and those who support dog fighting within the purview of the law. Enhanced punishments, stepped-up enforcement, and vigorous prosecution will help put an end to this violent and criminal activity.

Case in Point

In Texas, any gambling proceeds seized from a person convicted of dog fighting are forfeited and become property of the state.[32] And it is a crime to participate in the earnings, permit another to use property for a dog fight, attend a dog fight, or own or possess dog-fighting equipment.[33]

29. *Id.* § 2156 (2013).
30. *Id.* § 2156(g)(4) (2013).
31. *Id.* § 2156(e) (2013).
32. TEX. CODE CRIM. PROC. ANN. art. 18.18 (West 2013).
33. TEX. PENAL CODE § 42.10 (West 2013).

Animal Crush Video Law

Animal cruelty achieved a new level of depravity with the advent of crush videos. These videos appeal to people with a sexual fetish toward specific acts of animal cruelty that involve a woman, usually from the waist down, in a short skirt and stiletto heels or barefoot. She is usually talking seductively to the viewer, while torturing small animals, including small dogs, by crushing them with her feet. Sadly, these videos have been easily purchased via the Internet, and the first federal law making them illegal was found to be unconstitutional by the U.S. Supreme Court. The second law was challenged as well, although held constitutional by the Fifth Circuit Court of Appeals.

The source of these undercover videos is difficult to track. There are no faces shown, the filming locations can't be determined, and they are distributed over the Internet. In 1999, a federal law was passed criminalizing the distribution of crush videos, but the U.S. Supreme Court declared the law unconstitutional in the case of *United States v. Stevens*.[34] Congress then amended the law, carefully addressing the constitutional problems the Supreme Court raised in the previous law. However, the second law was also declared unconstitutional by a federal district judge in Houston when he dismissed most of the charges against a couple accused of heinous acts of cruelty to animals in crush videos. Federal prosecutors appealed the decision and the Court of Appeals for the Fifth Circuit reversed the district court, holding that the law was constitutional.[35] In the meantime, Houston's Harris County filed state animal cruelty charges against the couple.

The Fur Products Labeling Act

Would you buy a coat or a rug if you knew it was made of dog fur rather than faux fur? Probably not, and furthermore you would be angry at the manufacturer's deception. Protection from deceptions is one of the key roles of the federal government, and laws exist that mandate the inspection and monitoring of products we consume, use, and wear. The Fur Products

34. United States v. Stevens, 559 U.S. 460 (2010).
35. United States v. Richards, 755 F.3d 269 (5th Cir. 2014).

Labeling Act (FPLA) is one such law.[36] Originally passed in 1951, its purpose is to protect consumers from the misbranding or deceptive advertising regarding fur used in clothing and other products. The 1951 law contained various loopholes that were exploited by fur producers, and in 2009 the Truth in Fur Labeling Act was passed, amending the FPLA to close some of those loopholes.

Case in Point

(a) Introduction or manufacture for introduction into commerce, sale, advertising or offering for sale in commerce. The introduction, or manufacture for introduction, into commerce, or the sale, advertising or offering for sale in commerce, or the transportation or distribution in commerce, of any fur product which is misbranded or falsely or deceptively advertised or invoiced, within the meaning of this subchapter or the rules and regulations prescribed under section 69f(b) of this title, is unlawful and shall be an unfair method of competition, and an unfair and deceptive act or practice, in commerce under the Federal Trade Commission Act [15 U.S.C.A. § 41 et seq.].[37]

Dog fur has continued to enter the market, evidenced by a two-year investigation conducted by the Humane Society of the United States (HSUS) in 2012.[38] HSUS investigators purchased a vest, a pair of gloves, and a belt from a business in New York City, which was analyzed and found to contain fur from a domestic dog. HSUS urged greater compliance with and enforcement of the Dog and Cat Protection Act of 2000.

36. 15 U.S.C.A. § 69 (2014).

37. *Id.* § 69a(a) (2014).

38. HUMANE SOC'Y U.S., *Investigation by the HSUS Reveals Illegal Sale of Domestic Dog Fur in Apparel and Other Items*, http://www.humanesociety.org/news/press_releases/2012/07/investigation_dog_fur_071812.html (last visited Sept. 6, 2014).

Case in Point

Dog and Cat Protection Act Findings of Congress:

> (1) An estimated 2,000,000 dogs and cats are slaughtered and sold annually as part of the international fur trade. Internationally, dog and cat fur is used in a wide variety of products, including fur coats and jackets, fur-trimmed garments, hats, gloves, decorative accessories, stuffed animals, and other toys.
> (2) The United States represents one of the largest markets for the sale of fur and fur products in the world. . . .
> (3) Dog and cat fur, when dyed, is not easily distinguishable to persons who are not experts from other furs such as fox, rabbit, coyote, wolf, and mink, and synthetic materials made to resemble real fur. Dog and cat fur is generally less expensive than other types of fur and may be used as a substitute for more expensive types of furs, which provides an incentive to engage in unfair or fraudulent trade practices. . . .
> (4) Forensic tests have documented that dog and cat fur products are being imported into the United States subject to deceptive labels or other practices designed to conceal the use of dog or cat fur in the production of wearing apparel, toys, and other products.
> (5) Publicly available evidence reflects ongoing significant use of dogs and cats bred expressly for their fur. . . .
> (6) The methods of housing, transporting, and slaughtering dogs and cats for fur production are generally unregulated and inhumane.
> (7) The trade of dog and cat fur products is ethically and aesthetically abhorrent to United States citizens. Consumers in the United States have a right to know if products offered for sale contain dog or cat fur.[39]

The law states:

> It shall be unlawful for any person to—
> (A) import into, or export from, the United States any dog or cat fur product; or

39. S. JOURNAL, 106th Cong., Ch. 3, Sec. 1441 (Oct. 2000).

> (B) introduce into interstate commerce, manufacture for introduction into interstate commerce, sell, trade, or advertise in interstate commerce, offer to sell, or transport or distribute in interstate commerce in the United States, any dog or cat fur product.[40]

Knowing and intentional violations are fined at $10,000 for each separate violation; grossly negligent violations are $5,000 each; and negligent violations are $3,000 each.[41]

Also, individual states have an interest in animal welfare and protecting their consumers from fraud and have passed laws making it illegal to sell products that contain dog or cat fur. A violation under Virginia's law is punishable by a fine of not more than $10,000.[42]

The Americans with Disabilities Act and Service Dogs

The Americans with Disabilities Act (ADA) is a comprehensive and complex piece of legislation whose purpose is to prevent discrimination against people with disabilities, defined by the ADA as physical and mental impairments that substantially limit one or more major life activities, and to provide them with the same opportunities all Americans have in everything from housing to transportation to employment.[43] One of the ways that opportunities for the disabled are enhanced is through the use of service dogs or, as they are often now called, assistance dogs. A special bond exists between the person who is disabled and the dog (or in some instances another animal), which has been trained to perform certain tasks. The value of service dogs is implicitly ingrained in the ADA and related statutory schemes. Our law, in the civil rights context, attempts to translate this value into more inclusion while yet protecting the public.

The ADA is considered an equal opportunity law for people with disabilities. President George H. W. Bush signed the ADA into law in July 1990.[44] In stating the intent and purpose of the law, Congress found that

---

40. 19 U.S.C.A. § 1308(b) (2014).
41. *Id.* § 1308(c) (2014).
42. VA. CODE ANN. § 3.2-6589 (West 2008).
43. U.S. DEP'T JUSTICE, CIVIL RIGHTS DIV., *Information and Technical Assistance on the Americans with Disabilities Act*, www.ada.gov (last visited Sept. 6, 2014).
44. The ADA is a federal law. Titles I, II, III, and V of the law are codified in Title 42, chapter 126, of the United States Code, beginning at section 12101. Title IV of the original law is

discrimination against the disabled continued to be a problem in society even as legislative progress was made in other areas.[45] Unlike those who had experienced discrimination based on race, color, sex, national origin, religion, or age, the disabled had no legal recourse. This absence of a law resulted in exclusions from job opportunities, activities, travel, and other benefits enjoyed by Americans.

Today, individuals with disabilities are covered by a number of federal laws, most of which address service dogs in some manner. Section 504 of the Rehabilitation Act of 1973 applies to employers and organizations that receive financial assistance from any federal department or agency.[46] It forbids denying individuals with disabilities an equal opportunity to receive program services and benefits. The Rehabilitation Act preceded the ADA, and its limitations were in part the impetus for the passage of the ADA. The Air Carriers Access Act of 1986 (ACAA) prohibits U.S. air carriers from discriminating against individuals with disabilities.[47] The Fair Housing Act of 1968 and subsequent amendments protect the disabled from discrimination in housing.[48] And, in addition to federal laws, there are state laws that address treatment of those with disabilities.

Today, an extensive network of laws and implementing regulations protect the civil rights of the disabled and their service dogs. All of these laws, particularly those related to assistance dogs, have both commonalities and distinct differences. Understanding the various laws and how they work together can be confusing for the public.

The threshold issue to be determined is whether the individual has a disability under the ADA. A disability is defined as "a physical or mental impairment that substantially limits one or more major life activities of such individual; a record of such impairment; or being regarded as having such

codified in Title 47, chapter 5, of the United States Code. In 2008, the ADA Amendments Act was enacted to amend the existing law. The amendments made changes to the definition of the term "disability" and rejected the holdings of several Supreme Court decisions and portions of the Equal Employment Opportunity Commission's ADA regulations.

45. 42 U.S.C.A. § 12101(a) (2009).

46. 29 U.S.C.A. § 794(a) (2014).

47. 49 U.S.C. § 41705 (2014).

48. *A Consumer's Guide to Fair Housing*, http://www.hud.gov/offices/fheo/PIRC/DocumentsAbstracts/Iowa-Civil-Rights-Commission-R7/ICRC-FH-Consumer's-Guide/2007consumer'sguidetofairhousing.pdf (last visited Sept. 6, 2014).

an impairment."[49] Major life activities include, but are not limited to, "caring for oneself, performing manual tasks, seeing, hearing, eating, sleeping, walking, standing, lifting, bending."[50] Major life activities are also defined as "major bodily functions such as the immune system, normal cell growth, digestive, neurological."[51] The law includes rules of construction that explain how the definition is to be construed.[52]

We can see the impact of the law in many ways—ramps on public sidewalks and entrances, special rooms at hotels that accommodate wheelchairs, and elevators with Braille. And, of course, we see it in the use of assistance dogs, which evolved before the law but has expanded because of the protections afforded by the law. The original ADA defined "service animal" as a dog or "other animal" trained to do work or perform tasks for a person with a disability. This broad definition of "animal" and lack of clarity resulted in horses, monkeys, and even snakes being presented as service animals, creating obvious compliance problems for businesses, restaurants, and landlords. Therefore, new and updated requirements were put in place that limited service animals to dogs. As of March 15, 2011, under the Americans with Disabilities Act Title II (state and local government services) and Title III (public accommodations and commercial facilities), only dogs are considered service animals.[53] The service dog is further defined by the tasks she has been trained to perform. Examples include guiding the blind, alerting people who are deaf, pulling a wheelchair, and calming a person with post-traumatic stress disorder, among others. The rules are specific in that the dog's work or tasks must be directly related to the person's disability.[54] In addition to the exclusion of other animals as service animals, the revised rules specifically state that dogs who are used solely for emotional support are not service animals under the ADA.

If an individual is disabled and uses an assistance dog, places of business that serve the public, such as hotels, retail shops, and restaurants, are

49. 42 U.S.C.A. § 12102 (2009).
50. *Id.* § 12102(2)(A) (2009).
51. *Id.* § 12102(2)(B) (2009).
52. *Id.* § 12102(4) (2009).
53. There is a separate provision in the revised regulations about miniature horses.
54. U.S. DEP'T JUSTICE, *Service Animals*, www.ada.gov/service_animals_2010.pdf (last visited Sept. 6, 2014).

prohibited from discriminating against these individuals. State and local governments are also prohibited from discriminating against these individuals in the services they provide.

Case in Point

In *Sak v. City of Aurelia, Iowa*, James Sak, a permanently disabled retired police officer, sued the city of Aurelia, alleging that the city's failure to accommodate him and his service dog constituted discrimination and violated his civil rights under the ADA.[55] Sak's certified service dog, Snickers, was banned from the city of Aurelia because he was part "pit bull." (Pit bull is not a breed but a generic term used for a variety of dogs, including the American pit bull terrier and the American Staffordshire terrier.) The city had an ordinance banning pit bulls and refused to grant Sak an exception. In a lawsuit filed against the city, Sak and his wife, Peggy Leifer, requested, among other things, an immediate return of Snickers to Sak and a preliminary injunction against the city, enjoining it from prohibiting pit bulls with respect to Snickers. The city argued that the ordinance did not prevent Sak from having a service animal of a different breed, and that therefore it did not discriminate. The court disagreed, granting the preliminary injunction based in part on a "national public interest in enforcement of the ADA"[56]

Service dogs are special under the law. If a service dog is killed or injured, there may be specific laws that elevate the crime and/or provide for enhanced penalties. In Texas, Section 42.091 of the Penal Code, Attack on Assistance Animal, makes it a third-degree felony to kill an assistance animal.[57] It also provides for restitution, including for veterinary bills, for the cost of replacing the animal, or for the cost of retraining an injured assistance animal.[58] And in civil cases in states where market value is the measure of damages,

55. Sak v. City of Aurelia, Iowa, 832 F. Supp. 2d 1026 (2011).
56. *Id.* at 1026, 1047.
57. TEX. PENAL CODE § 42.091(c)(3) (2013).
58. *Id.* § 42.091(d) (2013).

the value of a service dog is going to be significant, given the training and skills of the dog.

To complicate matters, other federal laws and state laws may, and do, define "service animals" more broadly. The Fair Housing Act and Section 504 of the Rehabilitation Act of 1973 contain broader definitions of "assistance animal."[59] Housing providers are required to provide reasonable accommodations for an assistance animal that provides emotional support, as well as physical support, contrary to the ADA's provision.

The ACAA defines a service animal as "[a]ny animal that is individually trained or able to provide assistance to a qualified person with a disability or any animal shown by documentation to be necessary for the emotional well being of a passenger."[60] With respect to emotional support animals, although carriers may require documentation to verify that an animal is an emotional support animal, such documentation is not required by law.[61]

Unfortunately, one of the consequences of the broader use of service animals is the proliferation of imposters. In order to respect the privacy of the disabled, under the ADA a business may ask only two questions: (1) Is the dog a service animal that is required because of a disability? and (2) What work or task has the dog been trained to perform? The business cannot ask about the person's disability, require medical documentation, require a special identification card or training documentation for the dog, or ask that the dog demonstrate its ability to perform the work or task.[62] For emotional support animals, the airlines may request documentation and/or seek advance notice under the ACAA.

Limits on questions that can be asked, the introduction of emotional support animals, and the easy access via the Internet to "service dog" paraphernalia (dog vests, backpacks, ID cards, etc.) have made it relatively easy for individuals to break the law, sometimes unwittingly. And while it is a federal crime under the ADA to use an "imposter," recognizing and curbing

59. HUD guidance can be found at http://www.fairhousingnc.org/wp-content/uploads/2013/05/HUD-FHEO-2013-01-Service-Animals-and-Assistance-Animals-PWD-in-Housing-and-HUD-funded-programs.pdf (last visited Sept. 6, 2014).

60. Non discrimination on the basis of disability, 79 Fed. Reg. 41488 (emphasis added).

61. 14 C.F.R. § 382.23 (2009).

62. U.S. DEP'T JUSTICE, *Service Animals*, www.ada.gov/service_animals_2010.pdf (last visited Sept. 6, 2014).

abuse is difficult. States are beginning to address the problem, but those with disabilities worry about privacy and the safety of their dogs. There are no simple answers, and stakeholders have yet to agree on a solution.

FOR EVERYONE: If you are associated with a business or other entity that regularly deals with these issues, it is vital that you know the law. Employees must know the appropriate questions to ask and under what circumstances the business can refuse access to services. Seek the advice of a lawyer in understanding the complexities of the law.

State Laws

Most laws that protect dogs and humans are found at the state and local levels. Restrictions and regulations are passed under the police power of the state, with the purpose of protecting public health and safety. Governments must have valid reasons for imposing regulations and restrictions on their citizens, and health and safety is a valid purpose. As you will see as you go through this book, the power of the state is extensive, governing the practice of veterinary medicine, animal shelters, dangerous dogs, vaccinations, and more. Any animal issues that are specifically relevant to a state's agenda are covered, such as commercial breeding, roadside sales of animals, and consumer fraud. The laws also have various exemptions for such activities as hunting; they may exclude certain jurisdictions, such as smaller towns or rural areas; or they may exempt groups or professionals, such as veterinarians.

When looking for laws that regulate dogs, go first to the state laws. These laws provide the statewide, big-picture legal regime in your state. These laws may be found under any number of categories—agriculture, criminal, property, health and safety, consumer, or all of the above. With Internet access, it should be relatively easy to find the laws in your state that are important to you and your dog.[63]

63. The Animal Legal and Historical Center is an excellent legal resource for lawyers and for anyone who is interested in laws about animals. The site is supported in part by the Michigan State University College of Law and is one of the largest legal websites devoted to animal issues, and it is free. Visit the site at http://www.animallaw.info.

The investigation, implementation, and enforcement of state laws will fall to different entities, from animal control officers to the local police, state sheriffs, and even humane organizations. Penalties vary as well, from citations and small fines to jail time. Learn more about state laws in chapter 3, "The Legal Basics of Dog Ownership," and in chapter 4, "When Problems Arise."

Local Ordinances

Once you understand the state laws that apply, go to your city's local ordinances to learn what laws govern your specific city or county. Usually these ordinances are easy to find on a city's official website. Cities will often have an "animal" category of ordinances.

Chapter 3

THE LEGAL BASICS OF DOG OWNERSHIP

Now that you know what laws apply and where to find them, let's move on to the legal basics of dog ownership. Whether you have a dog or not, with approximately 83 million of them living with us, you are likely to share a sidewalk, an apartment wall, a neighborhood, or a home with a dog.[1] That means everyone should know the basics of dog law. Knowing the legal basics can be the difference between an unhappy neighbor and an ever-ready next-door "dog sitter."

Most of the relevant laws are found at the state and local levels and should be easy to find via the Internet. In addition to laws and ordinances, the various businesses and organizations that touch our dogs in some manner have their own rules and policies. Condominiums, gated communities, and apartments have rules, regulations, and policies regarding dogs. So if you are thinking of a new dog, do your homework up front—before you bring Buster home only to learn that he is over the weight limit allowed by your apartment complex.

1. Pets by the Numbers, HSUS, at http://www.humanesociety.org/issues/pet_overpopulation/facts/pet_ownership_statistics.html (last visited September 21, 2014).

A New Dog

Today, you can adopt a dog from a rescue group or shelter, giving a homeless dog a second chance and yourself a lifelong friend. Regardless of whether you want a puppy, a specific breed, or a dog with spots, you can find a great dog through a rescue group or shelter. In 2012, approximately 20 percent of the dogs owned in the United States came from shelters.[2] That leaves 80 percent still purchased from breeders, over the Internet, in retail stores, or in other ways.

The laws covering the purchase (or adoption) of dogs and related disputes vary by state and can fall under contract laws, consumer protection laws, property laws, and more. If you are beginning to think that you may need a lawyer to help you understand an adoption agreement or sales contract, do not worry; there are steps you can take to be informed and to understand what is involved in bringing home a new member of the family.

Rescue Groups and Shelters

The words "shelter" and "rescue group" are sometimes used interchangeably, but for our purposes, shelters refer to municipal shelters that operate on city funds and must take all dogs that are relinquished. Rescue groups are 501(c)(3) nonprofit organizations that rely on volunteers and operate largely with donations from the public. Both rescue groups and shelters are not in the business of breeding dogs for sale, but they are in the business of finding homes for dogs who are given up or abandoned.

Most rescue groups and shelters use the term "adoption" rather than "sale" in their agreements. "Adoption" is obviously a gentler word than "sale." It elevates the status of our companion animals and instills a greater sense of responsibility in the adopter, both of which are good motives. Given that "adoption" is a defining element in the contract, it is important for rescue groups, shelters, and adopters to understand what the word means legally under their state's law. Otherwise, it can create confusion because dogs are property, and in states such as Texas, property (dogs) cannot be legally "adopted" as children are adopted.

2. *Id.*

But doesn't the contract say "adoption"? Yes, it does, and some courts may find that the parties are free to contract using whatever terms they agree to use. And to a certain extent, that is true. As long as the adoption contract is never challenged legally or questioned, the adoption will stand. However, if the parties end up in a dispute, it becomes a bit more complicated. A judge's decision will likely be based on that state's legal principles that govern the sale and transfer of property, not adoption. Therefore, rescue groups and shelters need to understand how adoptions are viewed under their states' laws and be ready to explain it to all new adopters. And adopters need to be prepared to ask questions and to take the time to understand the terms of the agreement.

Other requirements and provisions in adoption contracts will vary by organization, but they all should be clear and understandable. Spay/neuter requirements, following the state's animal laws, and various disclosures and waivers are all part of an adoption contract. Separately, advice on care and any specific needs of the dog may also be included.

The role of shelters, and their relationship with rescue groups, is being reexamined in part as a result of a growing concern on the part of animal advocates regarding the number of animals being euthanized at shelters. Questions are being asked regarding what can be done to increase adoptions rather than euthanization. As with many animal protection issues, strong opinions are involved, along with some disagreements and controversy. Some animal advocates complain that shelters do not turn over animals to rescue groups or do not turn them over quickly enough, and that shelters do not make enough of an effort to encourage adoption of animals, such as extended hours, website promotions, and so on. Shelters reply that they are understaffed and underfunded and must take all animals that are relinquished, making it impossible keep animals long-term and to engage in additional efforts to promote adoption. Disagreements aside, states and municipalities are beginning to look more closely at their euthanasia rates. Tasks forces are being formed to analyze the data and present ideas for increasing adoptions. State laws and local ordinances have been passed that require shelters to transfer dogs to rescue groups quickly, extend their hours, and engage in additional efforts to find owners in order to save dogs' lives. In addition to the laws that are passed, states and cities must allocate the funds to support the laws that are enacted, if these efforts are to be successful.

Case in Point

Delaware's current law was passed in 2010 and requires the following:

> (a) Animal shelters shall be open to the public after normal business hours, including evenings and weekends, to increase access for the purpose of adoption. . . .
> (d) Animal shelters shall establish and maintain a registry of organizations willing to accept animals for the purpose of adoption, including breed specific rescues, or to provide the animals with long-term placements.[3]

FOR EVERYONE: Think ahead and do your homework before adopting a dog. It is a serious and long-term commitment.

- The more information you give to a rescue group regarding your home and family situation, the less likely you are to adopt a dog who will not fit your lifestyle.
- Get a copy of the contract, read it, and ask questions in advance. When the kids are jumping up and down with joy and the dog is licking your face is not a good time to go over the contract.
- Do not make assumptions and do not sign until you understand and are comfortable with the contract's provisions. Reviewing the contract in advance allows time to ask questions and receive answers.
- Do not sign a contract if there are obligations you cannot fulfill. Discuss changing the contract in a way that works for both you and the rescue group.
- Know as much about the dog as possible and your rights in the event the adoption does not work out. Often a rescue dog has no known history, but good rescue groups vet their dogs and often place them in foster care for a time before placing them in permanent homes.

3. DEL. CODE ANN. tit. 3 Agriculture, pt. VI, ch. 80, § 8003 (2010).

- Know what will happen if the dog has problems adjusting or is sick. Rescue groups and shelters will usually want the dog returned to them and will include that provision in their contracts. Most rescue groups do not reimburse for medical expenses. They operate on small budgets and cannot afford to cover additional costs. They will take the dog back and provide medical help through their network, and they will not euthanize the dog unless it is the most humane option.

FOR RESCUE GROUPS: Seek the help of a local lawyer in drafting your adoption contract. It will be money wellIf your dog dies spent to have an enforceable contract that protects you and your dogs. Do not copy an adoption contract from the Internet and assume it is legal in your state. There are ways that the contract can be drafted that will protect you and the dog, as well as provide the adopter with a valid contract. Have the lawyer explain the provisions so that you can explain them to your potential adopters. It will save time and money in the long run.

FOR LAWYERS: While the term "adoption" makes everyone feel good, it may not be recognized in many courts. In Texas, dogs can be sold, leased, or given away, but not adopted. Legal provisions can be incorporated that will work for the adopter and the rescue group. Also, research the cases in your jurisdiction to learn how judges have decided these types of cases. Talk to other animal lawyers in and outside your state to learn how they handle adoption contracts.

The Hobby Breeder

There was a time when the term "dog breeder" meant people who loved their particular breed of dog and bred them as a hobby, for enjoyment, and as a way to share their wonderful dogs with others. Although they sold their dogs, profit was not their main motivation. These hobby breeders learned about proper breeding and canine health and nutrition, and they took great pride in every litter of pups. They did not over-breed their dogs, and when puppies arrived they carefully scrutinized every potential owner.

The prospective owner was always welcome, and encouraged, to visit the breeder's home or facility where the dogs were kept, and potential owners always met the mother dog, her puppies, and sometimes the father of the litter. The future owner would make several visits and spend time with the entire litter of pups, deciding, with input from the breeder, which bundle of fur to take home when she was old enough to be separated from the mother and siblings.

There are still breeders who meet this description, and if you are set on buying a puppy from a breeder, be sure to find this kind—because the puppy business now has a dark side, and it's called a puppy mill.

The increase in dog ownership and our desire for immediacy has spawned an industry of large-scale breeders whose motivation is economic, with little or no concern for the welfare of the dogs. In puppy mills throughout the country, and outside the United States, female dogs spend their entire lives in small wire cages stacked three to four high, having litter after litter of puppies to feed the market. In addition to the obvious cruelty associated with puppy mills, the dogs that come from these "factories" may be diseased, may have genetic disorders, or may have temperament issues.

Reputable breeders who care for their dogs will allow you to see their facilities and will spend as much time as necessary with you to make sure you will be a responsible owner. They will tell you the good and bad of the breed and make sure you understand that having a dog is a long-term commitment.

Breeders will have sales contracts that specify the conditions of the sale and what they will and will not cover. They will be similar to rescue group contracts, and the points made in that section are relevant here. Breeders will include the situations under which they will take a dog back or exchange a dog. Unlike rescue groups, breeders will set out provisions regarding whether you may breed the dog if you are buying a puppy. The sales contract is a legal document that is governed by state and local laws. The sale may also be covered by a puppy lemon law if the state has one.

Breeders may also provide health certificates, pedigrees, and guidelines related to the care of your new dog. Read everything carefully and make sure you understand your legal obligations and the breeder's. Ask questions. Are you allowed to breed the dog? What guarantees are given? What recourse do you have if the dog has a health problem? Make sure everything is written into the contract. Do not depend on verbal agreements.

FOR EVERYONE: If a breeder will not allow you to see the facility, walk away. It may mean nothing, but do not take the chance that the dog has been bred and born under unhealthy or poor circumstances. Seeing where the dogs live and are bred is a basic and valid request. Your willingness to walk away will go far in helping to improve the welfare of dogs.

The Pet Shop

There has been a decrease in the number of brick-and-mortar pet stores that sell puppies. The reasons include the public's increasing awareness of the cruelty of puppy mills, the proliferation of Internet sales, and the movement toward increasing adoptions from rescue groups and shelters. In order to accelerate the end of pet store sales, cities such as Albuquerque, Austin, and Los Angeles have banned the retail sale of dogs in pet stores. Some pet stores are voluntarily ending sales in an effort to curb dog overpopulation and eliminate the demand for puppies that are bred at puppy mills.

Case in Point

Albuquerque's pet store ban:

> Pet Stores shall not sell Companion Animals but may sell other living creatures including, but not limited to, fish, birds, rodents, insects, arachnids, reptiles and other Permissible Exotic Animals.[4]

Except in unusual circumstances, purchasing a dog from a pet store will not provide you with an opportunity to see where the dog was bred, the dog's mother, or the siblings. If this does not convince you to walk away, your decision will have to be based on the health of the puppy, the reputation of the pet store, and the contract. You should have the puppy examined by an independent veterinarian before you purchase. As with rescue groups,

4. ALBUQUERQUE, N.M., CODE § 9-2-3-12 Pet Store Permit or PSP, http://www.amlegal.com/nxt/gateway.dll/New%20Mexico/albuqwin/cityofalbuquerquenewmexicocodeofordinanc?f=templates$fn=default.htm$3.0$vid=amlegal:albuquerque_nm_mc.

shelters, and breeders, know your legal rights and obligations. Research the company and find the person in the store who is most knowledgeable regarding the dogs and the store's policies. Every guarantee should be in writing.

Internet Sales

The Internet contains a vast network of international and national sellers. While numerous laws apply to Internet transactions, the nature of the jurisdiction—cyberspace—makes oversight and enforcement of those laws problematic. While well-known online retailers have reputations to maintain, the many sellers of puppies have little to lose and much to gain through an unknown and anonymous approach. The process of buying goods and services has changed, and the traditional ways we learned of a business's reputation, such as visits to the store, word of mouth, and long-term service in the community, are often not there. Internet sellers that have no actual location or people you can meet face-to-face are difficult, if not impossible, to investigate or validate. It is simply not advisable to purchase a dog over the Internet unless there is substance behind the website.

If you purchase a dog over the Internet who dies or is sick with health issues or a genetic disease, you are generally covered by the same state laws that apply to purchases from a local breeder or retail store, but with one major drawback. If the dog has been shipped or delivered to you, the seller is likely to be located in a different state or even a different country. Hiring a lawyer in another state and traveling to that state for a lawsuit is costly as well as impractical for most individuals. And the seller may not appear in court. If you sue in your state, the chance that an out-of-state seller will appear to defend the lawsuit is even less likely. And while a default judgment in your favor sounds good, collecting from an out-of-state or out-of-the-country Internet seller who has sold you a defective puppy will be challenging, if not impossible. Even if you purchase a healthy dog, you will not know whether you contributed to the continued operation of a puppy mill.

The only benefit to the Internet is immediacy and convenience, which is good for buying shoes but not for buying a puppy. If the Internet seller offers to compensate you, it will likely be with another puppy. Most purchasers of a puppy with a genetic disorder do not want another puppy from the same seller with the same risk of a genetic defect. And the purchaser may have bonded with the puppy and spent thousands of dollars on her medical care. Shipping her back to what may be a puppy mill to be euthanized is not an option.

The good news is that the volume of complaints from consumers has prompted the federal government's Animal and Plant Health Inspection Service (APHIS) to revise its definition of "retail pet store" in the regulations of the Animal Welfare Act (AWA) in order to bring more sellers under the licensing and inspection requirements of the law. Internet sellers were claiming "retail" exemptions based on the previous definition in the AWA regulations. That definition was written 40 years ago when the Internet was not a factor. The original intent of the exemption was that retail establishments allowed buyers to see the puppies and observe them; hence buyers were able to make educated purchasing decisions. Internet sales do not provide that option and should not be included in the exemption.

FOR EVERYONE: The overpopulation of dogs is everyone's concern. Consider saving a dog by adopting from a rescue group or shelter. If you do purchase from a pet shop, do your homework to try to determine where the puppy came from and read the fine print on the sales contract. Be sure you know your rights and obligations if the puppy is diseased or has genetic defects. Internet sales without a location that you can visit behind the website are risky and not advisable for the purchase of puppies. For more on your legal rights in the event of problems, see chapter 4, "When Problems Arise."

Where You Live

If you live in a condominium or an apartment, does the management allow dogs? If yes, what are the rules? Is there a weight limit? Is an extra deposit or extra rent required? These are questions that have to be answered before you bring a new dog home.

Rentals

Rental properties may be privately owned or subsidized by state or federal governments. They are all subject to various federal, state, and local laws. Private apartments, particularly those in competitive markets, are increasingly opening up their properties to renters with dogs. With approximately 83 million dogs in the United States, apartments in certain cities are finding it difficult to reject renters who have four-legged family members.[5] The properties usually require additional and nonrefundable deposits or rent for dog residents.

If your apartment has a "no pets" policy in place, it can be difficult to convince the owners to make an exception. If they do it for you, they have opened the door to exceptions for others. But what happens if your apartment building that allows dogs is sold and the new owner no longer allows dogs? Or what happens when the current owner bans certain breeds or adds a "no pets" provision to your lease? The first step is to review your lease. If your lease gives the owners the authority to insert this new provision or if your lease has expired, you can try to make a personal appeal to the new owners. Hopefully there are other renters with dogs in the building, and you can make a unified effort to keep the existing policy in place or engage in mediation to try to resolve the issue out of court. If the owners are unwilling to negotiate, you will have to weigh the costs of hiring a lawyer to fight the change in your lease, finding a new home for your dog (not an option for most), or finding a new apartment. Legal challenges can be mounted against the property owner, and decisions can be favorable, as in the following case.

Case in Point

In *Young v. Savinon*, the new owner of an apartment house instituted a "no pets" provision when he purchased the apartments. State law in New Jersey, where the case was heard, has an Anti-Eviction Act that limits the causes for eviction but allows landlords to make "reasonable" changes in the terms and conditions of the lease. In this case, the renters with dogs proved to the judge through their testimony and that of a psychological expert that enforcement of the "no pets" provision would be unreasonable.[6]

5. Pets by the Numbers, HSUS, at http://www.humanesociety.org/issues/pet_overpopulation/facts/pet_ownership_statistics.html (last visited September 21, 2014).
6. 492 A.2d 385 N.J. Super. (1985).

Condominiums and Gated Communities

Condominiums and gated communities usually have homeowners associations (HOAs) with governing boards of directors and may have additional management and staff. The HOAs are regulated by state laws, including laws that are specific to nonprofit organizations and condominiums. HOAs also have governing documents such as declarations, bylaws, and rules and regulations that dictate everything from the color of your front door to the weight of your dog. Thir dog rules may include outright bans; restrictions on size, breed, and number; and provisions that allow them to evict your dog if she is aggressive, destructive, or noisy. Though not actual laws, these types of rules and regulations are valid and are generally upheld in court if found to be reasonable, so know what is required before you buy, and do not assume you can ignore the rules or hide the facts.

Case in Point

In *Dulaney Towers Maintenance Corp. v. O'Brey*, the O'Breys purchased a second poodle in violation of their condominium's rule that owners may have only one dog. The Court of Special Appeals in Maryland ruled in favor of the condominium, finding that the Dulaney Towers rule that limited owners to one dog was reasonable.[7]

What happens if your condominium HOA decides that your dog is a nuisance and must leave the premises, or if it bans pit bull and Rottweiler breeds, which you happen to own? People who move into condominiums generally do so with the knowledge that they are subject to these rules, but changing rules relating to dog ownership can be considered unreasonable. There are ways to challenge the rules, first by reviewing the governing documents. Did the HOA board have the authority and follow the bylaws and other governing documents, as well as proper procedures, in instituting the new rule? Did it comply with state and local laws? What prompted the change? Implementing

7. 46 Md. App. 464 (1980).

rule changes may require a homeowners meeting and/or a vote. Make sure the rules have been followed. Has there been a lapse between instituting the new rule and enforcement? If the HOA board has looked the other way or enforced selectively, it is open to challenge. Before seeking legal assistance, you can make an appeal to the HOA board, which is comprised of your neighbors. However, be careful if your dog has been a genuine problem and you have done little to correct it. Your neighbors may not be too accommodating if you have ignored any problems related to your dog.

Subsidized Housing

Some types of housing receive federal and state subsidies and are subject to different laws than privately owned properties. In 1983, under the National Housing Act, a law was passed that prohibits properties designated for the elderly or the handicapped from discriminating on the basis of pet ownership. These requirements are found in the Code of Federal Regulations and are outlined by the U.S. Department of Housing and Urban Development (HUD).[8] Any project that serves elderly or disabled persons and is either subsidized or insured by HUD is required to allow pets. However, there are health-care exceptions such as nursing homes, intermediate care facilities, and board-and-care homes and hospitals. Pet rules must be enforced, and pet deposits are allowed if they do not exceed $300.[9] In 1999, a law was passed that further prohibits discrimination for all tenants in federally assisted housing, not just in housing designated for the elderly or disabled.

Case in Point

Federal law states:

> A resident of a dwelling unit in public housing (as such term is defined in subsection I of this section) may own 1 or more common household pets or have 1 or more common household pets

8. Pets in Properties That Serve the Elderly or Handicapped, at http://portal.hud.gov/hudportal/HUD?src=/states/shared/working/r10/mf/petpolicy (last visited Sept. 22, 2014).
9. *Id.*

> present in the dwelling unit of such resident, subject to the reasonable requirements of the public housing agency, if the resident maintains each pet responsibly and in accordance with applicable State and local public health, animal control, and animal anti-cruelty laws and regulations and with the policies established in the public housing agency plan for the agency.[10]

Reasonable requirements include payment of a nominal fee, a limitation on the number of animals, size and weight restrictions, prohibitions on animals that are dangerous, and other relevant conditions.[11] Further guidance to federally assisted housing is available in the Public Housing Occupancy Guidebook.[12]

These federal laws recognize the human-animal bond and acknowledge the importance of the comfort that animals can provide. Some states have followed suit, passing similar laws that apply to state-supported housing. Check your individual state's laws to learn whether your state prohibits discrimination against dog owners in housing.

The Health and Safety of Your Dog

Now that you are the proud owner of Fifi, or perhaps Fifi is the proud owner of you, what steps do you have to take to make sure she is a law-abiding dog? Many laws and ordinances apply to dog ownership, and they are centered on two main objectives: protecting the health and safety of the public and protecting the health and safety of your dog.

Licensing and Registration

Many cities require dog owners to register their dogs with the city and to obtain licenses. The cost is usually minimal and in addition to complying

10. 42 U.S.C.A. § 1437z-3.
11. *Id.*
12. Public Housing Occupancy Guidebook, at http://www.hud.gov/offices/pih/programs/ph/rhiip/phguidebooknew.pdf (last visited Sept. 22, 2014).

with the law, it's an extra layer of protection in the event your dog is lost. Further, while the law may not require it, microchipping your dog is a good idea. A tiny microchip about the size of a grain of rice contains ownership information and is inserted underneath the skin between your dog's shoulder blades. This technology allows your dog to be identified with a simple scanner, which is a standard item at most municipal shelters and veterinarian offices. This one act could save the lives of many dogs who are lost and assumed abandoned while their owners are desperately looking for them.

Case in Point

In September 2014, a Jack Russell terrier named Gidget, whose home is in Philadelphia, was found outside Portland, Oregon, 3,000 miles away. Missing for almost five months, Gidget was found by a good Samaritan and identified through her microchip.[13]

Tattoos are also a more permanent option. Greyhounds are tattooed and registered, and most can be traced back to their breeders. Collars can be removed and tags lost, but microchips are implanted and invisible.

Vaccinations

Vaccinations benefit our dogs and the public. Rabies has not been totally eradicated, although raccoons, skunks, bats, and foxes are the cause of most cases in the United States.[14] However, rabies vaccinations are always required. If your dog bites someone, he will be quarantined, either at home or at another location designated by the city, to determine whether he has rabies, regardless of whether you have proof of current vaccinations. Other vaccinations may not be legally required but can save your dog's life. Know what is recommended and the benefits and associated risks with the various vaccinations available.

13. Dog Found 3,000 Miles Away to Be Flown Home, at http://www.reuters.com/article/2014/09/20/us-usa-dog-oregon-idUSKBN0HF00T20140920 (last visited September 21, 2014).
14. http://www.cdc.gov/rabies.

Spaying and Neutering

An increasing number of cities require dogs to be spayed or neutered unless the owner is granted an exception. The goal is to reduce the number of births and the thousands of unwanted dogs that end up in shelters and are needlessly euthanized. In addition, cities see it as a public safety issue, as research studies show that the majority of serious dog bites are from intact dogs (dogs that have not been spayed or neutered). Some cities simply require payment of an additional fee to own an intact dog, or they allow exceptions for breeders. Also, as an alternative to an outright breed ban, some cities require that all "pit bull" dogs be spayed or neutered. Regardless of the law in your city, it is a good idea to spay or neuter your dog. Obtain the advice of your veterinarian, but for most dogs it is a low-risk procedure. And low-cost clinics and special programs are found in almost every city.

Adequate Care

Today, animals have greater legal protection than ever before, thanks to the work of animal advocates. With the tragedy of animal cruelty brought into the public conscience, lawmakers have responded with greater animal protection laws. In most cities, ordinances and state laws require you to provide basic care for your dog—food, water, and shelter.

Case in Point

In Michigan:

> (a) "Adequate care" means the provision of sufficient food, water, shelter, sanitary conditions, exercise, and veterinary medical attention in order to maintain an animal in a state of good health. . . .
> (h) "Neglect" means to fail to sufficiently and properly care for an animal to the extent that the animal's health is jeopardized. . . .
> (j) "Shelter" means adequate protection from the elements and weather conditions suitable for the age, species, and physical condition of the animal so as to maintain the animal in a state of good health.
> (k) "State of good health" means freedom from disease and illness, and in a condition of proper body weight and temperature for

Continued

Case in Point *Continued*

the age and species of the animal, unless the animal is undergoing appropriate treatment.[15]

States such as Arizona, California, and Texas, where the temperatures can reach 100+ degrees for days, have bans on tethering your dog outside and leaving your dog in a hot car. On a 90-degree day, the temperature inside a car can reach as high as 160 degrees in ten minutes.[16] A dog can die in a hot car in 15 minutes.

Case in Point

California is serious about the safety of dogs in cars, with a fine and possible jail time for violations.

> (a) No person shall leave or confine an animal in any unattended motor vehicle under conditions that endanger the health or well-being of an animal due to heat, cold, lack of adequate ventilation, or lack of food or water, or other circumstances that could reasonably be expected to cause suffering, disability, or death to the animal.
> (b) Unless the animal suffers great bodily injury, a first conviction for violation of this section is punishable by a fine not exceeding one hundred dollars ($100) per animal. If the animal suffers great bodily injury, a violation of this section is punishable by a fine not exceeding five hundred dollars ($500), imprisonment in a county jail not exceeding six months, or by both a fine and imprisonment. Any subsequent violation of this section, regardless of injury to the animal, is also punishable by a fine not exceeding five hundred dollars ($500), imprisonment in a county jail not exceeding six months, or by both a fine and imprisonment.

15. MICH. COMP. LAWS ANN. § 750.50 (2001).
16. Dogs in Hot Cars, at http://www.peta.org/issues/companion-animal-issues/cruel-practices/dog-hot-car (last visited Sept. 22, 2014).

> (1) Nothing in this section shall prevent a peace officer, humane officer, or an animal control officer from removing an animal from a motor vehicle if the animal's safety appears to be in immediate danger from heat, cold, lack of adequate ventilation, lack of food or water, or other circumstances that could reasonably be expected to cause suffering, disability, or death to the animal.[17]

States have other safety laws, such as prohibitions on transporting dogs unsecured in the beds of pickup trucks and open vehicles; tethering a dog; and overworking a dog. Check individual state and local laws for the ones that apply to you.

In addition to laws regarding basic care, state anticruelty laws prohibit the abuse of your dog, whether intentional or unintentional. All states have felony animal cruelty laws, which can mean jail time. See chapter 5, "Animal Cruelty and the Law."

Dog Insurance Policies

While pet insurance is not a legal requirement, it is becoming more popular as dog owners consider ways to insure the health and longevity of their companions.[18] Owning a dog can cost thousands of dollars—the first year alone. Would you be able to afford the veterinary bills if your dog sustained any of the injuries below?

- A Labrador puppy collided with a 55-gallon tortoise aquarium, shattering the tank and lacerating the puppy, requiring surgical staples.[19]

---

17. CAL. PENAL CODE § 597.7 (2006).
18. Julie I. Fershtman has contributed this section on pet insurance. She is a shareholder at Foster Swift Collins & Smith, PC, in Michigan, and practices equine law, insurance law, and business litigation. She is a former vice-chair of the ABA TIPS Animal Law Committee and past president of the State Bar of Michigan. For more information on Ms. Fershtman, visit www.equinelaw.net and www.equinelawblog.com.
19. Caterina Pontoriero, *America's Most Unusual Pet Claims*, PROP. CASUALTY 360 (June 25, 2012), http://www.propertycasualty360.com/2012/06/25/americas-most-unusual-pet-claims.

- An English cocker spaniel devoured a bowl of raisins and almonds, toxic to dogs, requiring that his stomach be pumped and an almond surgically dislodged from the back of his sinuses.[20]
- A large, powerful snowy owl snatched a 15-pound Jack Russell terrier from his back yard and dropped him from the sky into a neighbor's yard. The dog's injuries included deep lacerations, a skull fracture, and bruising of his lungs, kidneys, and liver.[21]

These events really happened, and the owners were spared massive veterinary expenses, paying only few hundred dollars. How? They had pet insurance policies.

As you evaluate whether pet insurance is right for you, make sure you understand how it works, your responsibilities, and what pet insurance policies do and do not cover.

An Overview of Pet Insurance

Pet insurance policies are designed to offer coverage for veterinary expenses if your dog suffers an accident or illness.[22] Some policies also cover certain routine maintenance expenses. A typical policy can cost more than $29 a month,[23] but your cost will depend on your dog's age, breed,[24] level of desired coverage, and other factors.

Is Pet Insurance Right for You?

Opinions differ on the value of pet insurance. In 2011, *Consumer Reports* published an opinion that "most pet owners would be better off passing up pet insurance and instead putting some money in an emergency 'kitty.'"[25]

20. *Id.*
21. *Ashburn Pup's Snowy Owl Attack Cited as Most Unusual Pet Insurance Claim*, LEESBURG TODAY, Feb. 26, 2014, http://www.leesburgtoday.com/news/ashburn-pup-s-snowy-owl-attack-cited-as-most-unusual/article_3040162c-9f05-11e3-8f74-001a4bcf887a.html.
22. These policies are known to be held by less than 4 percent of pet owners in the United States. *See Pet Healthcare Insurance*, ABA-TIPS ANIMAL LAW COMMITTEE NEWSLETTER, Spring 2008, at 13.
23. *2013 Pet Insurance Cost Analysis*, PR NEWSWIRE (Nov. 12, 2013).
24. One report notes that the most expensive dog breed to insure is the English bulldog. *Id.*
25. *PET Insurance*, CONSUMER REP. (Aug. 2011), http://www.consumerreports.org/cro/magazine-archive/2011/august/money/pet-costs/pet-insurance-rarely-worth-the-price-in-our-analysis/index.htm.

Still, pet insurance is becoming increasingly popular, and about 3 percent of dog owners in the United States have purchased this coverage.[26]

The following chart weighs the advantages and disadvantages of pet insurance.

The Pros and Cons of Pet Insurance

Pros	Cons
Dogs are prone to a variety of accidents, and if a dog sustains a significant injury, pet insurance can potentially provide needed funds to finance surgical procedures, medications, and care. In essence, it might save your dog's life by providing funds to cover very costly veterinary attention. Depending on the policy, you might be covered for surgical care and follow-up attention for serious conditions such as hip or elbow dysplasia. The policy might even cover behavioral conditions for which a veterinarian prescribes expensive medication. Some policies cover wellness visits for vaccinations and inoculations and sometimes spay/neuter surgery. Some policies cover alternative therapies for your dog such as acupuncture or chiropractic care. Because policies list their exclusions, you can review the policy before buying the coverage to determine whether it excludes services or conditions that might be important to you.	Policy limits apply, but companies might offer you the option to purchase higher policy limits. Expect the policy to include a deductible that you pay for each claim, which might amount to 20 percent of the claim (depending on the policy's terms). Often, per insurance company, policies have a waiting period after their effective date, during which you cannot make certain types of claims. Some policies exclude specific congenital defects such as patellar luxation, umbilical hernias, elongated soft palates, mitral valve defects, and malocclusion. Depending on the policy, exclusions can also apply to hereditary conditions, even those of which you were unaware but that manifested after the policy took effect. If you bought a puppy of a breed with an elevated risk of a condition, such as hip dysplasia, even though the puppy has shown no signs of a problem, it is possible that the policy will not cover this risk. Read the policy carefully before buying coverage.

26. *Pets Best Insurance Services*, PROP. CASUALTY 360 (March 18, 2014).

Know Your Obligations

Read the fine print. Pet insurance policies, just like any insurance policy, impose obligations and deadlines. For example, you will need to report claims to the insurer (or the insurer's designated representative) within time limits and in a manner that the policy requires. Also, you will need to keep, and submit with your claim, records of your dog's covered expenses.

Disputes Involving Pet Insurers

Like any contract, pet insurance policies can be the subject of disputes and litigation. Options for resolving disputes with insurers include submitting a complaint to the state insurance bureau and filing a lawsuit.

State Insurance Bureau Complaints

Insurance companies receive extensive regulation from state and federal governments. Policyholders who have legal disputes with insurers can consider submitting a complaint with a state bureau that handles consumer complaints, such as the California Department of Insurance,[27] the Texas Department of Insurance,[28] the Colorado Department of Regulatory Agencies,[29] or the Illinois Department of Insurance.[30] For more information on filing a complaint against an insurance company, visit the National Association of Insurance Commissioners at http://www.naic.org

Litigation

Policyholders may also have grounds to file a lawsuit against the insurer, even if they already filed a complaint against an insurance company or broker through a state regulatory agency. Depending on the applicable state law, an insurer can be sued under several possible legal theories such as breach of an implied covenant of good faith and fair dealing, bad-faith treatment of an insured party, breach of contract, and possibly others.

27. http://www.insurance.ca.gov.
28. http://www.tdi.texas.gov.
29. http://cdn.colorado.gov/cs/Satellite/DORA/CBON/DORA/1249686120221.
30. http://insurance.illinois.gov.

No known reported court rulings exist to date related to pet insurance policies. By comparison, considerable case law exists involving equine (horse) and livestock insurance disputes. Lawyers who represent pet owners are encouraged to review these cases for possible similarities. For example, cases addressing "sound health" at the policy's inception might offer some guidance to counsel evaluating disputes over preexisting conditions.[31]

Public Health and Safety

We have just covered laws and ordinances that govern the health and safety of your dog. The following are focused on the health and safety of the public.

Dogs Running Loose

Everyone has heard of the "pack mentality" and when dogs are running freely and unrestrained, they can form packs with other dogs, which can make them more aggressive and dangerous to humans. Most cities have leash laws that prohibit allowing a dog to run loose, but dogs are still found roaming some neighborhoods, which can threaten the safety of people and dogs. Having your dog on a leash also means you have greater control over the dog in the event she becomes frightened.

Number of Animals

More cities are passing ordinances limiting the number of dogs you may keep in a single residence. Noise and sanitation issues have prompted the passage of these types of ordinances. Rescue groups and breeders that are located in cities are being affected negatively by the ordinances, but they may be allowed exemptions or grandfathered in. While the restrictions are still relatively new, groups that are challenging them are learning that the courts are finding the ordinances constitutional.

31. *See Animal Insurance Litigation, in* LITIGATING ANIMAL LAW DISPUTES: THE COMPLETE GUIDE FOR LAWYERS 341 (Joan E. Schaffner & Julie Fershtman, eds., 2009).

Case in Point

In *Holt v. City of Sauk Rapids*, the plaintiff argued that the ordinance limiting the number of dogs was unconstitutional. The court stated in its decision that to prevail [in a constitutional challenge], appellants must show that the lack of any rational relationship between Sauk Rapids' ordinances limiting the number of dogs per residential unit and the public health, safety, or general welfare is not even debatable. They do not meet this burden; therefore, the ordinances cannot be held unconstitutional.[32]

Nuisance Laws

While you may like the fact that your dog barks when someone comes to the door or walks down your alley, a dog that barks constantly can be an annoyance to your neighbors, especially if there are common walls, such as in high-rise buildings and apartments. Local ordinances and state laws prohibit creating a nuisance, which includes a barking dog, or the law may be specific to barking dogs. The criteria for what constitutes a nuisance will vary. It may be barking for a certain length of time, such as 15 minutes; or it may be in accordance with a "reasonable person" standard; or, it may be left to the animal control or law enforcement officer to investigate and determine whether your dog's barking is a nuisance. If your dog's behavior is creating a problem for your neighbors, take steps to correct it. There are several humane solutions once you determine when and why the dog barks. If you have a new dog, it could be a temporary situation until he becomes familiar with his surroundings. If not, a dog trainer can help determine why the dog barks and how to resolve the problem.

If you are the neighbor who is bothered by a barking dog, first contact the dog's owner. The dog may bark only after the owner leaves, meaning that the owner doesn't know about it or assumes you are not bothered by it. Some neighbors feel safer if there is a dog barking nearby. If that approach does

32. 559 N.W.2d 444 (Minn. Ct. App. 1997).

not work, sometimes a letter from a lawyer will prompt action. Otherwise, contact the appropriate enforcement authority—your landlord, HOA, or city enforcement section. You should have a record of when the dog barks and for how long and know the ordinance or rules that apply.

Another nuisance in urban living is dog waste. Cities require that you clean up after your dog, although some owners still ignore the law. It is vital that owners clean up after their dogs, particularly in urban environments, for health and aesthetic reasons, and more importantly to be a responsible citizen and dog owner. Dog waste has become such a serious problem that some communities are taking matters into their own hands.

Case in Point

Cities, HOAs, and apartment complexes are turning to a new method of enforcement of waste pick-up: DNA testing. Dog owners are required to register their dog's DNA with a cheek swab, and waste left in the streets is collected and analyzed. If it is your dog's waste, you may be fined or the waste may be returned to you for disposal.

Violations of most animal ordinances are misdemeanors, which are considered minor crimes or misdeeds. A citation will usually require that you comply with the law and/or pay a fine to the city. Be aware that some of the fines can be significant. Allowing Buddy to run off-leash in a public park may be fun for him, but it may come at a steep financial price. If you are cited for a violation such as registration and you were actually in compliance, you can appear and present proof of registration, and the charge may be dismissed.

Ordinances, like state laws, will have exceptions and exemptions. Police dogs, service dogs, and hunting dogs are exempted from certain laws. Individuals and groups such as breeders, dog trainers, veterinarians, and animal control officers are also exempt from certain laws but are required to comply with others. Even cruelty laws will not apply to certain individuals and situations.

Taking Your Dog with You

With our dogs having family member status, we should be able to take them everywhere, right? We are actually moving closer to that goal, with more facilities, such as hotels and restaurants, realizing the public relations and economic benefits of allowing dogs in their establishments. Certified service dogs are given broad access to facilities by law (see the discussion in chapter 2 on the Americans with Disabilities Act), but our mixed-breed rescues, if well behaved, are gaining ground.

The Park

Many cities have established dog parks, which are fenced-in areas where dogs can run and play off-leash, a treat for friendly dogs who spend their days indoors or tethered to their owners by a leash. Some dog parks have two areas, one dedicated to smaller dogs and the other for big ones. While the leash laws do not apply, all other laws do, and you are responsible for controlling your dog's behavior while in the park.

Airplanes and Trains

If you want to take your dog with you when you fly, the safest place for her is in the cabin with you. Your dog must be small enough to fit in a carrier under the seat in front of you. So although Bubba, your drooling 120-pound bullmastiff, thinks he is a Chihuahua, you will have a hard time convincing a flight attendant that he could fit under the seat. The inability to place your dog under the seat inside the airplane means that your options come with additional risks that you have to understand and evaluate fully before choosing to transport Bubba by airplane.

The airlines establish their policies regarding baggage and the transport of pets. Bubba is property when he flies, just as he is in other situations, and he is considered a type of checked baggage if he is not traveling in the cabin with you. Failure to plan in advance and read the fine print can result in devastating consequences.

Case in Point

In *Gluckman v. American Airlines, Inc.*, Andrew Gluckman traveled to Phoenix, Arizona, a trip that was a high school graduation gift from his parents. During a camping trip, a young golden retriever wandered into camp and attached himself to Gluckman, who named the dog Floyd. When returning home, Gluckman, who had never purchased an airline ticket, was told that Floyd would have to travel in the baggage compartment. Gluckman claimed that the agent made no disclosures regarding possible dangers: that the cargo hold was not air-conditioned, that the hold could not be monitored, or that the temperature could exceed the airline's own safety limits. Floyd died of heat stroke when the temperature in the baggage compartment reached 140 degrees.[33] Gluckman sued for emotional distress and loss of companionship, claims that were dismissed by the court.

Gluckman's situation may have had a happy ending if he had known to do the following:

- Plan in advance. Packing a dog is not like packing your swimsuit, or even taking your children, who travel alongside you.
- Know it is your responsibility to do your homework. Do not depend on the airline to tell you everything you need to know.
- Thoroughly review the airline's website regarding its policies on the transportation of pets.
- Talk to the airline regarding any questions. Know what happens to your dog every step of the way—from the time you part company until you meet at your destination.
- Visit other reputable websites that have tips regarding traveling with your pet.[34]

33. 844 F. Supp. 151 (1994).
34. *See e.g.*, http://www.humanesociety.org/animals/resources/tips/traveling_tips_pets_ships_planes_trains.html?credit=web_id110483989#airplane (last visited Sept. 22, 2014).

- Talk with your veterinarian about issues that may be distinct to your dog. Some dogs are less heat tolerant or may be anxious. Make sure your dog has all of the necessary vaccinations and identification.
- Make sure the weather is suitable. The airlines have restrictions, but again do your homework.
- Consider other options if your dog cannot travel in the cabin with you. Companies that specialize in transporting dogs can transport your dog in air-conditioned comfort.

Airlines are required to report statistics on animals that are lost, injured, or die in transit only if they are classified as pets. They are not required to report statistics on commercial shipments, such as breeders. That rule changes as of January 1, 2015, when U.S. Department of Transportation rules will require airlines to report statistics on commercial shipments as well.[35]

For international travel, check the U.S. State Department rules on "Pets and International Travel" ahead of time to ensure you follow proper procedures.[36] You will find more extensive rules and regulations regarding travel outside the United States, or to the state of Hawaii, which has special regulations regarding quarantine. If you are traveling to a foreign country, check its policies regarding quarantine and vaccinations.

Pets are not allowed on trains unless they are service animals. However, in May 2014, the city of Chicago launched a pilot program to allow train travelers to take small dogs and cats with them. Check with the train operators to see what their policies are regarding pets.

Restaurants

Dogs are found inside restaurants in Europe, but except for service dogs, they are not allowed in restaurants in the United States. However, some restaurants have outdoor patios where dogs can sit with their owners. Restaurants

35. Report by Air Carriers on Incidents Involving Animals During Air Transport, at http://www.regulations.gov/#!documentDetail;D=DOT-OST-2010-0211-5439 (last visited Sept. 22, 2014).
36. Pets and International Travel, at http://www.state.gov/m/fsi/tc/c10442.htm (last visited Sept. 22, 2014).

are usually required to apply for special permits to allow dogs on the patio, so don't assume all patios will take dogs. And make sure your dog is well behaved around tables of food.

The Workplace

Research has shown that having dogs at work can boost morale and lead to greater teamwork, but most employers have yet to jump on the bandwagon. That may change as they see that they may be missing out on more productive workers.

Case in Point

Fortune magazine reported on a recent study by researchers at Central Michigan University that suggests that employees in workplaces with dogs might also engage in higher levels of collaboration and ethical behavior.[37] The 120 individuals who participated in the study scored higher overall on measures of trust, team cohesion, and intimacy when dogs were present.

The report goes on to say that with policies in place to ensure the animals are clean and friendly, pets may promote wellness and enhance overall satisfaction in the organization.[38]

The challenges that arise when there are dogs in the workplace concern employees who are afraid of dogs, who simply do not like them, or who are allergic to dog fur. These issues will have to be addressed before there is an open-door policy for dogs in the workplace.

Pet-Friendly Hotels

Traveling with your dog can be great fun, and it is becoming easier as more hotels are opening their doors to dogs. Even five-star hotels and resorts are

37. Take Your Dog to Work Day is today, for real, at http://fortune.com/2013/06/21/take-your-dog-to-work-day-is-today-for-real (last visited Sept. 22, 2014).
38. *Id.*

allowing four-legged furry guests if Mimi, your finicky Maltese, travels only first class. To learn whether a hotel accepts dogs, simply check its website. There are also specific websites and mobile apps that list pet-friendly hotels as well as restaurants and dog park locations.

And if Mimi needs a break from the pressures of keeping her humans happy, there are pet spas and hotels that provide five-star services including massages and gourmet meals.

Chapter 4

WHEN PROBLEMS ARISE

Life is fraught with problems. Dog ownership is no exception, although most dog owners agree that the benefits of a companion animal greatly exceed any problems that may arise. And they will also agree that the problems that do occur are usually human, rather than canine, in nature.

This chapter presents some of those human acts that may affect the lives of you and your dog and some of the options for resolving problems.

If a New Dog Has Problems

Shelters and Rescue Groups

If you adopt a dog from a shelter or rescue group, you have usually agreed to take the dog "as is," a legal term meaning that there are no warranties or guarantees and that you accept the dog in his current condition. Most rescue groups have vetted their dogs for temperament and behavioral issues and will report anything notable—good and bad. It is to their advantage to make sure you know the dog's behavior before you adopt. But as a prospective adopter, you should always ask about the vetting process if the rescue group does not mention it. And know that the dog's history may be unknown. Also, the dog has probably been examined by a veterinarian, given all vaccinations, and spayed or neutered if old enough. She may have spent an extended period with a foster parent. Despite these precautions, it is always possible that your new dog may have some behavioral issues or short-term problems adapting to a different environment.

The first step in the event of a problem is to review your adoption agreement and any other documents that you signed and/or were given. Know what the terms of the agreement are, then contact the rescue group or shelter. Rescue groups and shelters want you to be satisfied and want to find the right home for their dogs, and they will work with you or take a dog back if she is not adapting well. They can often help with behavioral issues if you do not want to return the dog. If you do return the dog, unless there are major problems, they will keep him until they find the right forever home; meanwhile, they will try to find another dog for you, one who is comfortable with you and your lifestyle. Whether you are entitled to the return of the adoption fee will be indicated in the contract. However, the money you give has usually been spent on veterinary fees, food, and care for the dog, so do not expect to receive a refund.

If the dog has health problems, the adoption agreement usually specifies what type of veterinary medical reimbursement, if any, is provided. A resolution will depend, in part, on the dog's illness or disease and when it occurred. Again, talk to the rescue group or shelter. Some organizations have relationships with veterinarians who can treat your dog for certain problems.

Retail Sales by Breeders and via the Internet

Given that retail sales usually involve puppies rather than adult dogs, the legal issues are most often related to purchases of puppies who have genetic defects; who die shortly after purchase from serious illnesses, such as parvovirus; or who have other health problems. The owner who purchases one of these puppies may spend a significant amount of money on veterinary medical expenses and will seek reimbursement from the seller.

Additional problems with purebred dogs can include temperament problems, breed-specific defects, or the inability of the dog to perform the job trained for, such as hunting or protection.

If you have signed a contract with the seller, start with what you and the seller have agreed to in the contract. While it seems obvious, buyers, in their excitement over a new puppy, may not read the contract, or even if they do, they may sign it without question. Retail sellers and breeders usually agree to replace puppies under certain conditions, which include specific steps that must be taken by the purchaser, including returning the sick puppy. Breeders may not cover veterinary fees and if they do, there are specific requirements such as how soon to report a problem and which veterinarian to use. And expect the breeder to personally have the dog examined. Failure to follow the requirements will void the contract provision, which is usually stated. Often the owner has already spent money on veterinary expenses and has become attached to the dog, so return is not an option. Dogs with genetic defects who are returned to breeders are often euthanized, which owners may find unacceptable if other options are available. Contract provisions can be challenged under certain situations, and purchasers should consider having a lawyer review the contract for potential challenges if the breeder or retail establishment is unwilling to resolve the issue.

The purchase may be covered by consumer protection laws, puppy lemon laws, or other laws in the state where the purchase was made. If significant funds have been spent, a consultation with a lawyer is advisable in order to understand what options are available and the associated costs. California's puppy lemon law allows a purchaser, under certain conditions, to return, exchange, or keep the dog and to be reimbursed for reasonable veterinary fees.

Case in Point

California ill or diseased dog; remedies of purchaser

(a) If a licensed veterinarian states in writing that within 15 days after the purchaser has taken physical possession of the dog after the sale by a pet dealer, the dog has become ill due to any illness that existed in the dog on or before delivery of the dog to the purchaser,

Continued

Case in Point *Continued*

or, if within one year after the purchaser has taken physical possession of the dog after the sale, a veterinarian licensed in this state states in writing that the dog has a congenital or hereditary condition that adversely affects the health of the dog, or that requires, or is likely in the future to require, hospitalization or non-elective surgical procedures, the dog shall be considered unfit for sale, and the pet dealer shall provide the purchaser with any of the following remedies that the purchaser elects:

(1) Return the dog to the pet dealer for a refund of the purchase price, plus sales tax, and reimbursement for reasonable veterinary fees for diagnosis and treating the dog in an amount not to exceed the original purchase price of the dog, plus sales tax.

(2) Exchange the dog for a dog of the purchaser's choice of equivalent value, providing a replacement dog is available, and reimbursement for reasonable veterinary fees for diagnosis and treating the dog in an amount not to exceed the original purchase price of the dog, plus sales tax.

(3) Retain the dog, and reimbursement for reasonable veterinary fees for diagnosis and treating the dog in an amount not to exceed 150 percent of the original purchase price of the dog, plus sales tax on the original purchase price of the dog.

(b) If the dog has died, regardless of the date of the death of the dog, obtain a refund for the purchase price of the dog, plus sales tax, or a replacement dog of equivalent value of the purchaser's choice and reimbursement for reasonable veterinary fees in diagnosis and treatment of the dog in an amount not to exceed the original purchase price of the dog, plus sales tax, if either of the following conditions exist:

(1) A veterinarian, licensed in this state, states in writing that the dog has died due to an illness or disease that existed within 15 days after the purchaser obtained physical possession of the dog after the sale by a pet dealer.

(2) A veterinarian, licensed in this state, states in writing that the dog has died due to a congenital or hereditary condition that was diagnosed by the veterinarian within one year after the purchaser obtained physical possession of the dog after the sale by a pet dealer.[1]

1. CAL. HEALTH & SAFETY CODE § 122160 (1995).

There is a separate penalty to the seller as well.

Case in Point

California: Diseased or defective dog; sale; penalties

> [N]o pet dealer shall knowingly sell a dog that is diseased, ill, or has a condition, any one of which requires hospitalization or surgical procedures. . . .
> An action for recovery of the civil penalty and for a court order enjoining the pet dealer from engaging in the business of selling dogs at retail for the period set forth in this section, may be prosecuted by the district attorney for the county where the violation occurred, or the city attorney for the city where the violation occurred, in the appropriate court.[2]

Laws such as California's have been enacted in response to the growing incidence of consumer complaints and the inadequate remedies available when individuals purchase sick dogs. If you buy from a breeder, the best defense against buying a sick or defective puppy is to meet the breeder in person, see the facility, know your rights, and meet your puppy's family before you buy.

If you have purchased a defective puppy from an Internet seller with only a telephone number and a website, you are not in a good legal position. It is likely that the seller may be in a different state or country. Filing a lawsuit in a different state, or even in a different city of your state, presents numerous challenges. See chapter 3, "The Legal Basics of Dog Ownership." I have included the potential hazards of the Internet in that chapter in order to warn you before you buy.

If you know the location of the seller and do not want to file a lawsuit, you can consider filing a complaint with the attorney general in that state. Attorneys general play an active role in protecting consumers in their states. It is possible that there are other complaints and that the state will

2. *Id.* § 122205 (1995).

investigate and possibly act on your complaint. While you may never get your money back, you can try to protect the next unsuspecting buyer.

Case in Point

I received a call from a young woman who had purchased a puppy over the Internet. The Internet site was not specific to a breeder but was a general site where people sell everything from auto parts to engagement rings. The puppy had parvovirus, a highly contagious virus in dogs that causes diarrhea, vomiting, and often death. This dog died after the young woman had spent a significant amount of money on veterinary expenses, and she wanted to know what she could do. My first question was jurisdictional. Where was the breeder located? She did not know. I then asked her whether she had a contract. Her answer was no. In fact, all she had was a telephone number and, not surprisingly, the seller was not returning her telephone calls. This young woman had virtually no practical recourse at this point. Do not make this mistake. For any chance of a remedy, it is best to purchase a dog in or near the city where you live. While some Internet sellers will make good on their claims, the risks and inconvenience to you and the dogs are greater given the circumstances.

Ownership Disputes

With an estimated six to eight million unwanted dogs and cats in shelters every year and with three to four million of those being euthanized, one cannot help but marvel at the contentious and often expensive legal battles waged over the custody of a divorcing couple's dog, who may be a 12-year-old, diabetic, blind beagle.[3] It seems paradoxical, but it is actually a testament to the strength of the human-animal bond and the unique nature of our companion animals. Unlike the property designation dogs have been given under the law, they are far from mere property in the minds of those couples fighting for custody.

3. HUMANE SOC'Y U.S., http://www.humanesociety.org/animal_community/resources/qa/common_questions_on_shelters.html (last visited Sept. 6, 2014).

Ownership disputes arise in a variety of situations and if the parties cannot agree, a resolution may involve litigation or other settlement avenues. Family law judges find themselves wrestling with ownership claims in divorces and breakups. Dogs that are presumed to be abandoned are given new homes only to have their original owners appear and sue for their return. Crises, such as the disaster surrounding Hurricane Katrina, create an entirely new set of complex issues regarding ownership and animals in disaster situations.

Family Law Custody Disputes

Custody issues arise in family law cases when two people who have lived together are separating and both are claiming ownership of the family dog. If a couple cannot agree, they may look to the courts to decide ownership in divorces, partnership splits, and other relationships in which they have shared their lives and a dog. Unlike other personal property such as a car, a dog is unique and cannot be easily replaced. It is not realistic to sell the dog and divide the proceeds (although I know of a judge who threatened to do just that). And, of course, that is not what the parties want. A ten-year-old Labrador retriever with hip dysplasia may have a negative cash value, but he is priceless to the divorcing husband and wife fighting for possession.

As you have seen so far, dogs are in an unusual position in our legal system. While legally considered property, they are arguably much more than property to most owners. Nowhere is that more evident than in custody disputes. The law and the courts are starting to adapt, although slowly, to the idea that our companion animals lie somewhere between property and children, with opinions at both ends of the spectrum. With other animals such as livestock, monetary settlements can usually be agreed to because there is an economic value, and sentimental attachment may not be a factor. And with children, the laws regarding custody are clear, and children may be old enough to express their wishes. Parties fighting for custody of a dog will find themselves at the mercy of the case law in their state, if there is any, and of the judge's view on how these cases should be resolved.

Although animal lawyers and advocates have urged it, courts have yet to fully embrace a "best interest" analysis as used in child custody disputes.

Cases exist, but they are sporadic.[4] Some judges utilize a traditional property analysis, considering any reference to "custody" to be "flawed."[5] While legally sound, a traditional property approach is unsatisfactory in many ways; one is that it fails to consider the essential reason that the matter is before the courts—the parties do not consider their dog property. Most cases are hybrids, with judges considering "best interest" factors such as caring for the dog's needs (e.g., walking and feeding), and "property" factors such as licensing and registration.

Case in Point

In *Travis v. Murray*, Judge Matthew F. Cooper of the Supreme Court of New York County felt it necessary to disclose his personal situation ("I own a dog, a rescued pit bull mix named Peaches."[6]). He acknowledges the challenges typified in his custody case of Joey the dachshund.

> [C]ourts are left with little direction with respect to questions surrounding dog custody: Can there be such a thing as 'custody' of a canine? . . . While the dog owners of New York might uniformly regard their pets as being far more than mere property, the law of the State of New York is in many ways still largely at odds with that view.[7]

Noting that these types of disputes "will only increase in frequency," the judge grants a full hearing, noting that "the parties may need to address questions like: Who bore the major responsibility for meeting Joey's needs . . . ?[8]

The law and legal precedent control when judges decide cases, which means that the court cases will trend toward property concepts, albeit, complicated

4. *See* Placey v. Placey, 51 So. 3d 374 (Ala. Ct. Civ. App. 2010). The Alabama court uses the term "best interests" in a dog custody case.
5. *See* Clark v. McGinnis, 298 P.3d 1137 (Kan. App. 2013).
6. Travis v. Murray, 977 N.Y.S.2d 621 at 625 n.1 (N.Y. Sup. Ct. 2013).
7. *Id.* at 625.
8. *Id.* at 631.

ones. If the dog is registered with a kennel club or organization, has a microchip, or is registered with the city, an owner will be listed. Adoption or sales contracts may also be used, as may proof that the dog was a gift. Veterinary bills may be presented, although payment alone is not necessarily sufficient. Beyond documentation, evidence of who actually cared for the dog on a day-to-day basis—who provided him with food and water and walked him—may be considered. If children are involved, the person who has custody of the children may have an advantage if the children are attached to the dog. Witnesses, such as neighbors, may be allowed to testify as to who walked and cared for the dog.

FOR EVERYONE: As in most situations, it is advisable to try to reach an agreement outside the courtroom. If an agreement cannot be reached, ask your lawyer about possible mediation before having the court decide. Consider a mediator who has training and specific experience in animal-related issues.

FOR LAWYERS: Family law issues are emotional, and a couple fighting over a dog is no exception. If the parties cannot come to a resolution without going to court, it is important to determine what cases are relevant in your jurisdiction. Case law exists, so if there are no cases in your jurisdiction, review what is available in other jurisdictions and choose the strategy that is best for your client and the dog. Know whether mediation is a viable option for your client and the court. Consider presenting property and custody evidence in order to advance the law and to encourage a move beyond a traditional property analysis in these types of cases.

If the Rescue Group Wants the Dog Back

Ownership disputes with rescue groups usually occur when a rescue group claims the adopter has breached the contract and attempts to take the dog back and/or files a lawsuit to obtain the dog. Rescue groups usually include provisions in their contracts that allow them to take the dog back or compel the adopter to return the dog under certain circumstances, such as evidence of cruelty, misrepresentation on the application/agreement, or failure to comply with other conditions of the contract. Notwithstanding cruelty, which may be a criminal matter, the alleged right to take back a dog in this situation raises a number of legal issues, not the least of which are the questions of who owns the dog, whether the rescue group retains an ownership interest, and what that interest entails.

Case in Point

In *Frank v. Animal Haven, Inc.*, the plaintiff brought a personal injury suit against the shelter for injuries suffered in a dog bite. The plaintiff claimed that the shelter maintained an ownership interest in the dog based on the contract having a return provision. The court disagreed, finding that Animal Haven's "right to have the dog returned if Skimbiraushkas breached the contract's provisions . . . was clearly to protect the well-being of the dog, not to reserve ownership."[9] This court narrowly construed the contract provision in this case and what the shelter intended.

Can the rescue group take the dog back? The answer, as in most legal situations, is that it depends. Any number of factors may be determinant, including the specific facts, the state's laws, any case law on the subject, the language of the contract, and the intent of the parties. However, it is unlikely that a judge will view this as an "adoption" as in family law but rather will look at contract and property laws to determine the character of the transaction and the associated rights.

FOR EVERYONE: The best approach is to prevent finding yourself in this situation. Do your homework in advance and be clear on your responsibilities and those of the rescue group before you sign the contract. See chapter 3, "The Legal Basics of Dog Ownership."

If the Municipal Shelter Has Your Dog

Municipal and county shelters operate differently from rescue groups. As government entities, shelters must comply with specific state laws, city ordinances, and numerous policies and procedures that govern municipal and state entities. Unlike a rescue group, whose sole mission is to save dogs and

9. Frank v. Animal Haven, Inc., 967 N.Y.S.2d 370 (2013).

adopt them, a city shelter must serve many purposes and has little discretion in some areas. It must accept all dogs relinquished by owners and dogs in cruelty cases who have been taken by animal control or other entities charged with these responsibilities.

The ownership dispute most likely to arise is when a family dog escapes and is taken to the city shelter by animal control or someone who has found the dog. The shelter should check for a registration, microchip, tattoo, collar, tags, and any other indications of ownership. If the shelter checks, and you have identified your dog, you and your dog will most likely be happily reunited.

Problems arise if your dog has no identification, if he has been lost, or if the shelter fails to check and your dog is considered ownerless. If you do not find your dog and claim him within a certain length of time, based on most local and/or state ordinances and policies, you will lose title to your dog, and the shelter will become the dog's owner.

Case in Point

Dogs are property, which means you have constitutional rights to your dog. If your city ordinance or state law does not specifically say that ownership transfers to the city, the legal answer may not be so clear. In Houston, Texas, a German shepherd was impounded by Houston's animal shelter and adoption facility. After the required three-day hold policy of the shelter, the dog was transferred to a rescue group. The original owners came forward and asserted ownership after the dog had been transferred. The rescue group claimed ownership based on proper impoundment and transfer from the city's animal shelter. The original owners sued for the return of the dog. The trial court found that the original owners retained title to the dog because Houston's local ordinance contained no provision that terminated original ownership in the dog after the hold period. The trial court decision was reversed on appeal, although for reasons other than Houston's lack of a provision terminating ownership. Houston had best resolve this issue before it occurs again.

The City of Dallas ordinance states: "If an animal is not redeemed within the appropriate time period specified in Subsections (b) through

Continued

Case in Point *Continued*

(d), **the animal will become the property of the city** and may be placed for adoption, euthanized, or otherwise disposed of as recommended by the director."[10] The city of Dallas is clear on the transfer of ownership in cases of abandoned or lost dogs.

Hold periods are usually short (typically 72 hours), given that most city shelters are usually overcrowded and have to move dogs in and out of the shelter quickly. However, in certain parts of the country, animal shelters are not overcrowded and have people waiting to adopt dogs. Efforts are being made to transport dogs from overcrowded shelters to these locations. There are a number of nonprofit organizations that transport dogs, as well as pilots who are willing to fly them at no cost.

Once the hold time expires, the shelter will either turn your dog over to a rescue group, attempt to adopt your dog, or euthanize your dog if no one adopts her or if she has health or behavioral issues that make her unadoptable in the opinion of the shelter. While it may not seem fair that the shelter obtains ownership so quickly, the shelter's position is that it cannot keep dogs indefinitely. Shelters have tight budgets, making it difficult to devote additional resources to determining whether a dog has an owner. Most dogs are relinquished voluntarily, so the shelter must try to find new owners or, sadly, must euthanize the dogs who are not adopted within a certain time period.

What happens if you discover that the shelter or the rescue group has allowed someone else to adopt your dog, and you want him back? If the adopter is unwilling to return the dog to you, you have few options other than to file a lawsuit. And you may not learn the name of the adopter unless you file a lawsuit. Rescue groups and shelters will not readily release the names of their adopters or go back to the adopter on your behalf.

Your likelihood of success in court will depend on a number of factors, starting with the facts. Under what circumstances did your dog end up at

10. DALLAS, TEXAS, CITY CODE § 7.2-6(e) (2013) (emphasis added).

the shelter? What efforts did you make to find your dog? How long was your dog missing? Did your dog have identification? Did the shelter miss the microchip?

Legally, the judge will decide which laws should apply to the facts. Is the law or ordinance constitutional, and did the shelter adequately follow the law? Was there a valid transfer of title from one party to the next? Is there an agreement between the shelter and the rescue group? Did you legally abandon your dog? Does the law of lost and abandoned property apply? What are the rights of the adopter, who did not know there was an owner at the time? The legal issues are complex and it is advisable to seek the assistance of a lawyer to develop a strategy to make a strong case, regardless of which side you are on.

FOR EVERYONE: Unless your dog never leaves the house, it is always possible that she could escape or become lost. The best way to help ensure that your dog is returned is to microchip her, register her with the city if applicable, and give your dog a dog tag with your contact information. These are the best ways to ensure that your dog will be returned to you.

FOR LAWYERS: If you have a client whose dog was taken by a shelter, the best advice is to work with a lawyer who has handled these types of cases. The case law is sparse and the issues complex.

Finders Keepers

What if you find a dog wandering the street and decide to take her home? She looks healthy and well fed but has no identification. In an effort to find a possible owner, you have her scanned for a microchip, post signs in the neighborhood, list the dog on relevant websites, and call the local shelter asking if anyone is looking for her. It is important, for more reasons than one, to make a diligent effort to find the owner in this situation. The most important reason is to try to prevent someone's heartache of losing a beloved companion animal. And, your efforts will be relevant if you want to keep the dog or give her to someone else.

Six months later no one has come forward. You still have the dog and have become quite attached to her, have given her the name Duchess, and consider her to be yours. What if the original owner shows up a year later and demands her return? Perhaps the owner was out of the country and unaware that the dog had escaped from the boarding facility or family who was caring for her. You have to decide whether or not you want to return Duchess to her original owner. You can make that decision based on your personal assessment of what occurred, but it is best to consult a lawyer. If you decide to keep her, you may find yourself the defendant in a lawsuit. The judge will ask many of the same questions asked in the shelter case just discussed. What are the facts, and what laws apply? Decisions go both ways.

There is never a win/win when two people love the same dog. What happened to the residents and their animals in Hurricane Katrina exemplifies the challenges and heartaches that can accompany the loss of a dog and the legal battles that can ensue in the effort to get that dog back.

Case in Point

The intense and drastic effort to evacuate the residents of New Orleans during Hurricane Katrina resulted in thousands of dogs and cats left stranded. Rescue workers refused to allow residents to take their animals, at times forcibly removing people from their homes when they refused to leave their dogs.

The documentary film "Mine" chronicled the efforts to save the surviving animals left behind and the stories of four New Orleans residents who tried to reunite with their dogs after the dogs had been placed in other homes.[11] One dog was resettled in California and was gladly returned to the original owner when the facts were discovered. Another dog was returned thanks to the efforts of a compassionate individual with the support of a pro bono law firm. One dog was found but was never returned to the original owner. A German shepherd was given to a rescue group that found a new home for the dog; a legal battle ensued and the new owners retained ownership.

As you can see, there was one disaster and four distinct situations. There is no way to predict what will happen—inside or outside the courtroom. The

11. MINE, a film by Geralyn Pezanoski (2007) (DVD available at www.filmmovement.com).

same legal issues in the ownership fights for the Katrina dogs can be found in many lost-dog situations. Were the dogs actually abandoned under the law? What were the legal rights of the new owners who were not aware that the existing owners were looking for their dogs? What were the legal obligations and liability of the individuals and rescue groups that moved the dogs out of one state and placed the dogs in new homes without the knowledge of current owners?

FOR EVERYONE: If you find a dog and decide to return him, you want to be sure that you have returned the dog to his rightful owner, have complied with the law, and are free of any current and future liability. Consider seeking the advice of a lawyer if you have concerns. If you decide to keep the dog, you will need a lawyer to assess and defend your interests. There are always extenuating circumstances that could affect your legal case. A lawyer will be able to advise you.

FOR LAWYERS: While the finder may have made a valiant effort to locate the owner, and a great deal of time may have passed, the court may find that the dog is to be returned to the original owner. How much time has passed, the condition of the dog when found, and the care given by the finder may or may not be relevant. If your client is the finder and has become attached to the dog, prepare him for an adverse decision. Case law may be difficult to find, but precedent may exist that will either help or hurt your case, and you need to know about it.

Wrongful Death or Injury

Death or injury to your dog while in the care of another can happen in any number of situations. We entrust our dogs to veterinarians, dog walkers, and groomers. We give our dogs food and treats from product manufacturers that we assume make safe and healthy products. And our expectations are usually met. But at times, a moment of carelessness or an intentional act can result in mistakes that cause the death or injury of our beloved companions. In our grief and anger over a needless death or serious injury, we want answers, and we want to ensure that the same mistakes do not happen again. Tempers flare and the person accused becomes defensive, which makes it difficult to resolve issues without the help of a third party. And there are times that filing a lawsuit may be the only, or the best, option to pursue.

About Damages

Damages in animal-related lawsuits are a hot topic today in legal circles. Under the law, the purpose of awarding damages, other than punitive damages, is to compensate the injured party for the harm that has been done. A dog cannot be replaced, so winning a case of wrongful death means an award of money. Unless there is a crime, such as an act of cruelty, no one will go to jail over a negligent act. The purpose is not to punish the actor but to compensate the person harmed.

State laws and court decisions dictate the type and amount of damages that may be awarded in cases. Economic damages may include costs such as the market value of your dog, various expenses, or future expenses.

Noneconomic damages, such as pain and suffering, emotional distress, loss of consortium, and sentimental value are slowly making their way into companion animal wrongful death cases. Some states have passed statutory laws granting noneconomic damages while placing a limit on the amount that can be awarded.[12] Some states are creating legal precedent by awarding noneconomic damages in case law. As you learned earlier in this book, each state has its own laws, and nowhere is that more evident than in the way the states address animal issues.

Exemplary damages, also known as punitive damages, may be awarded in negligence cases if the defendant was grossly negligent or acted with malicious or willful intent. Some situations allow double or treble damages.

In some types of cases, attorney's fees may be awarded to the party that prevails. In these cases, lawyers may agree to work on a contingency basis, which means that they will take a percentage of any award. In the tainted food case that follows later in this chapter, the lawyers received their fees in the $24 million settlement. However, do not assume that lawyers can receive attorney's fees in all cases.

12. *See* TENN. CODE ANN. § 44-17-403 (2007). Tennessee has a $5,000 cap on damages.

In contract cases, the damages may be specified in the contract. For example, if Muffin is injured during a training session, there may be a provision in the contract regarding whether veterinary medical care will be provided, and if so, what type. A contract may also include a "specific performance" provision, or a judge may require specific performance in a lawsuit when a monetary award is not adequate to compensate the injured party. For example, rather than a reimbursement, a trainer may be required to keep working with Muffin until her behavior improves.

If your dog has been harmed and you decide to go to court, you have to determine what amount of money will compensate you, even if your dog has died. If the amount is small, you may file suit and represent yourself in a small claims court. For example, the small claims courts in Texas are authorized to handle cases with amounts of $10,000 or less. If you are asking for something other than money, such as the return of your dog, or if a large sum of money is involved, you will generally need to hire a lawyer to represent you.

Veterinary Malpractice

Society's change in attitude about our companion animals has brought about a similar change in attitude about veterinarians. Today, veterinarians are closer than ever to human physicians in terms of what we expect in the treatment of our dogs. We take our dogs for yearly checkups and teeth cleanings while sometimes forgoing our own yearly checkups. We are more likely to treat our dogs for serious illnesses rather than euthanize them, and we use veterinarians who specialize in areas such as orthopedics and cardiology. There are 24-hour emergency clinics in the event that our dogs are injured or become ill when regular veterinarian clinics are closed. As a consequence, we are holding veterinarians to a high standard of care and are more likely to take action if we feel they have not lived up to our expectations. Depending on what sources you believe, veterinary malpractice appears to be on the rise, but that conclusion is not clear, as the American Veterinary Medical Association (AVMA) does not keep statistics on veterinary malpractice suits.

Veterinarians go through extensive medical education and training. Once in practice, they are held to the national standards of the AVMA and must adhere to state and local laws, such as business and health codes. States have veterinary medical associations and disciplinary boards that review complaints and conduct hearings when necessary. While each state has its own laws on veterinary malpractice, it is generally considered "professional" negligence and is legally similar to medical malpractice.

So how do you know whether your veterinarian was professionally negligent or whether the injury or death was simply unavoidable? It may be obvious. If your veterinarian operated on the wrong leg, the proof is evident. Most situations will not be so clear and will require the advice of experts—a lawyer and a veterinary medical expert. You will need to know whether you have a case, the strength of the case, what your damages may be, and how much it will cost you. It is usually legally complex and costly. Most veterinarians have malpractice insurance that provides them with lawyers to defend them. Filing a veterinary malpractice lawsuit without a lawyer is not advisable.

To prove your case in court, your lawyer will have to prove that through a negligent act or failure to act, your veterinarian caused injury or death to your dog. In most cases, you will have to prove four elements: (1) that your veterinarian had a duty to you (and your dog); (2) that the veterinarian breached that duty; (3) that the breach caused injury to your dog; and (4) that you suffered damages.

Veterinary malpractice cases are like medical malpractice cases in that you will have to submit evidence in the form of expert witness medical testimony, a necropsy (animal autopsy) report and/or other proof of the cause of death, and documentation to prove that the veterinarian's methods, treatment, or procedures were below the standard of care of other veterinarians in similar situations. The type of proof required will be dictated by the state. And you have to prove that the treatment actually caused the death or injury to your dog. Your veterinarian may have provided treatment that was below standard, but it may not have been the cause of death. You must be able to connect the treatment with your dog's injury. And finally, you have to prove that you suffered damages. In veterinary malpractice, your damages may be small. In many states, you are allowed only the market value of your dog, meaning that a 15-year-old mixed-breed dog may have little value in the courts. However, there has been a continual push for noneconomic damages such as sentimental value, and such cases are appearing, although infrequently.

Case in Point

In *Bluestone v. Bergstrom*, the plaintiff sued for veterinary malpractice in the death of his Labrador retriever mixed-breed dog. The jury awarded Bluestone $39,000 in damages, with $30,000 for market value and "special value" to the owner. The appeals court upheld the award.[13]

These types of cases exist, but they are rare. As an alternative to filing suit, or in addition to it, you or your lawyer may file a complaint with the licensing and disciplinary board in the state where your veterinarian practices. There will be a procedure for filing complaints, which are evaluated by an oversight board. If the board believes that your complaint warrants further investigation, the veterinarian may be required to present evidence, attend a hearing, and/or present her side of the story.

A Word of Caution

Some owners, in their grief and anger over the death of their dog, will turn to the Internet to express their opinions. The Internet is neither an open nor totally anonymous forum. You may open yourself up to a lawsuit and significant money damages if you make what the court finds is a defamatory statement on the Internet that harms a veterinarian or his practice. If you plan to make a public statement on the Internet or in any public forum, seek the advice of a lawyer to determine which statements are within your right to free speech and which statements may prompt a lawsuit against you.

13. Bluestone v. Bergstrom, No. 00CC00796 (Cal. Super. Ct. Orange Cnty.) (2003).

Case in Point

When my client was angry and discouraged over her veterinarian's failure to adequately address the death of her dog, she decided to protest at her veterinarian's office. It was her right to protest as long as she followed the law, which included knowing what the city required and what the U.S. Constitution allows. For example, she had to stay on public property. She had to make truthful statements. Her peaceful and lawful protest allowed her to deal with the death of her dog in a manner that worked for her, without subjecting herself to a defamation suit or illegally harming the veterinarian.

FOR OWNERS: If your dog dies, one of the ways you may prove malpractice is through a necropsy, or an autopsy on an animal, which can establish a cause of death. Do not allow your dog to be cremated or destroyed; otherwise the evidence has been destroyed. Also, necropsies must be done quickly to avoid deterioration of the body. If you think your veterinarian has committed malpractice, preserve the body and talk with a lawyer before filing suit. You need to determine the validity of your case and know the strengths and weaknesses, the cost to file suit, and what your damages may be if you win. Also, there are time limits, known as statutes of limitations, on filing suit. Talk with a lawyer to determine when you have to file.

FOR LAWYERS: If you have never handled a veterinary malpractice case, talk with a lawyer in your jurisdiction who has, if possible. There may be important issues in your jurisdiction of which you are unaware. For example, in Texas, a plaintiff who has not paid the veterinarian bill and loses the malpractice case could be faced with thousands of dollars in attorney's fees in the collection of that debt. Also, laws are changing constantly, and some states allow for sentimental or other noneconomic damages. Make sure you know what is available, and consider whether you and your client want to challenge the status quo in your state. Finally, in most states, dogs are worth very little in market value. Make sure you have fully disclosed the economic and legal realities to your client regarding noneconomic damages and the cost of trying a case, which can be significant.

Groomers, Boarding Facilities, Dog Walkers, and Trainers

With the growth of dog ownership, there has been an explosion of products and services we can purchase for our canine companions. Everything from raincoats to spa treatments to counseling is available to us at a price. Unfortunately, not all of these businesses are regulated or reputable; sometimes workers are not properly trained to do the job, and their negligence causes harm. When using a new service, it is always advisable to check it out personally, obtaining references and checking available resources for complaints.

Negligence

Groomers, boarding and training facilities, dog walkers, and other businesses provide an array of services to dogs and their owners. If the owners or employees negligently cause harm to your dog, the laws of contract, consumer protection, and/or negligence may apply. Veterinarians who provide commercial services beyond veterinary care, such as boarding, may fall under these legal concepts as well.

Common law negligence involves acting or failing to act in a manner in which a person of ordinary prudence would have acted under similar circumstances. Examples abound. If I do not give my dog water for several days, it is obvious that I am being negligent. A person of ordinary prudence would know that a dog should not go for several days without water.

The range of problems that may occur due to negligence varies widely, from minor grooming injuries to a dog's death from heat stroke at a boarding facility. Before filing a lawsuit, it may be to your advantage to try to negotiate a settlement with the facility. The owners may have insurance that will cover the damages, or they may be willing to write a check. Owners may not want bad publicity, and one of the provisions of a settlement is that you agree not to disclose the details of what happened and the settlement. You have to determine whether or not this requirement is acceptable to you.

If you cannot settle the case and you decide to file a lawsuit, you will have to prove that: (1) the defendant owed you a legal duty; (2) the defendant violated that duty; (3) the violation caused injury to you or your property; (4) the defendant's violation was the cause of the injury; and, (5) you suffered damages. The specifics of proving negligence will be based on the common law and/or state law where the injury occurred. Lawyers who handle personal injury cases are experienced in the law of negligence.

You may also choose to file suit in small claims court if the amount of money damages is small. Go to your city's official website and search the courts to determine whether small claims court is appropriate for you. There will be a limit on the amount claimed, but the courts are generally set up to allow plaintiffs to file suit without hiring a lawyer. Some legal processes will apply and you will have to submit evidence, but there should be instructions geared for the nonlawyer.

Bailment

A bailment is a type of contractual arrangement between two parties—a bailor and bailee. There are federal laws on bailment, but a case involving your dog will likely be based on state law. A nonanimal example of a bailment that we all recognize is the act of taking your clothes to the dry cleaner. You (bailor) leave your dirty clothes (your property) with the dry cleaner (bailee) with the expectation by both parties that you will pick them up cleaned and pressed. In the case of your dog, you deliver your dog Max to the groomer with the expectation that you will pick him up clean and fluffy. In Texas the basics of a bailment are (1) the delivery of property to a person (bailee) from the owner of the property (bailor) for a purpose (grooming of a dog); (2) acceptance of the property (the dog); (3) an express or implied contract between the parties regarding the purpose (dog is to be groomed); and (4) the understanding that the property (the dog) will be returned to the owner (bailor) with the purpose fulfilled (the dog will be clean and fluffy). In these types of bailments, you and the bailee benefit (Max is clean and handsome, and the groomer is paid). There may be no written contract that has been negotiated in advance, and ownership of Max does not change.

Lawsuits filed under bailment agreements may be resolved using contract law or negligence (tort law), depending on how the judge interprets the facts. Laws vary from state to state, and your damages, burden of proof, and other legal aspects of your case will be dictated by the specific laws in place and may depend on who benefited—the bailee, bailor, or both—and whether you were negligent as well.

A Contract

Another legal relationship is established through a contract. A contract can be oral or written, and it is either express (terms are expressly stated) or implied (terms are inferred from the circumstances). For example, you may enter into a contract with a dog trainer to teach Muffin how to sit, stay, and heel. Generally, valid contracts under state laws (such as those of Texas) will have an offer, an acceptance, a "meeting of the minds," consent by both parties, and execution and delivery with the intent that it be mutual and binding. A contract must be supported by consideration, such as the money you pay for Muffin's training. In addition to the payment, you may have obligations under the contract, such as showing up for some of Muffin's training sessions or buying certain equipment required for her success.

If you have a written contract, the legal dispute will usually be based on breach of contract. Either party may claim breach of contract. The contract will be the key evidence the court will use to decide your case. So, if you are asked to sign a contract, read it, ask questions, and understand what you are signing. Better yet, if significant money or property is involved, have a lawyer review it.

Consumer Protection and Breach of Warranty Laws

Consumer protection laws have been passed specifically to protect consumers who purchase defective goods or services or who are victims of fraudulent practices. If you have been sold goods or services that are defective or that you believe have been misrepresented, the law in your state may offer a remedy under a consumer protection law. The following provision from the Texas Deceptive Trade Practices Act is one cause of action in a "laundry list" of possible claims.

Case in Point

It is a violation of Texas's consumer protection law to represent that goods are "of a particular standard, quality, or grade, or that goods are of a

Continued

Case in Point *Continued*

particular style or model, if they are of another."[14] How might this apply to a special harness you bought that didn't work as claimed on the package?

Breach of warranty claims are another aspect of consumer protection laws that cover the purchase of defective products. In a breach of warranty, a seller has made a claim or representation about the quality of a product that was not fulfilled.

About Waivers

Boarding facilities, rescue groups, and trainers—virtually everyone—will require you to sign a waiver of liability holding them harmless in the event of certain events or accidents. We are all familiar with waivers when we bungee jump or go rock climbing. And you are generally given one choice in the matter—either sign or walk away. Waivers apprise you of the risks involved in whatever activity you plan to engage in or whatever service or product you are about to purchase. Waivers are not absolute and are closely scrutinized by the courts because they are not generally favored and may be against public policy. Consumers are often at a disadvantage when dealing with professionals and may not understand the extent to which they are relinquishing their rights. The following Texas law indicates what is, and what is not, acceptable in a waiver of consumer protection.

Case in Point

Texas Waivers: Public Policy

> (a) Any waiver by a consumer of the provisions of this subchapter is contrary to public policy and is unenforceable and void; provided, however, that a waiver is valid and enforceable if:

14. TEX. BUS. & COM. CODE ANN. § 17.46 (2007).

(1) the waiver is in writing and is signed by the consumer;
(2) the consumer is not in a significantly disparate bargaining position; and
(3) the consumer is represented by legal counsel in seeking or acquiring the goods or services.

(b) A waiver under Subsection (a) is not effective if the consumer's legal counsel was directly or indirectly identified, suggested, or selected by a defendant or an agent of the defendant.

A waiver under this section must be:

(1) conspicuous and in bold-face type of at least 10 points in size;
(2) identified by the heading "Waiver of Consumer Rights," or words of similar meaning; and
(3) in substantially the following form:

> "I waive my rights under the Deceptive Trade Practices-Consumer Protection Act, Section 17.41 et seq., Business & Commerce Code, a law that gives consumers special rights and protections. After consultation with an attorney of my own selection, I voluntarily consent to this waiver."[15]

Angry Neighbors

Disputes with neighbors who are unhappy with your dog's barking, killing the grass, or chasing their cat can quickly escalate and become serious. Who's right or wrong is largely irrelevant if the cat dies or your neighbor kills your dog. That is why it is best to try to resolve these conflicts before the situation escalates. If you and your neighbor own your homes and don't plan to leave in the near future, it is obvious why you should try to work it out. If you can't talk with each other, mediation is a good option before calling the police or filing a lawsuit. Having a neutral third party in an emotional situation may be all you need to resolve the conflict. If mediation fails, go to the legal basics. Look up your city's local ordinance and see what it says about the problem. If the problem is barking, is your dog

15. TEX. BUS. & COM. CODE ANN. § 17.42 (1995).

in violation of the ordinance? If there is no specific ordinance on barking, look at your city's nuisance law. Is your dog being a nuisance? If yes, take action. The barking may not bother you, but a violation requires action on your part. Is your neighbor being unrealistic? What do other neighbors say?

If you live outside the city limits, look at your state's law. If you live in a very small town, there may be no law specific to your circumstances. It may fall to the county sheriff to mediate your dispute.

Some situations allow others to legally harm your dog. If your dog is attacking someone, the person being attacked has the legal right to defend herself or another person. In some jurisdictions, a person is allowed to shoot a dog who is bothering livestock. If your neighbor injures your dog without legal justification, then your neighbor has interfered with your property rights. Although your dog may have little market value, you may have incurred significant medical expenses and can represent yourself in small claims court or hire a lawyer in an effort to recoup your expenses.

Product Manufacturers

We like to believe that the products we buy from large manufacturers are safe and that they have been tested thoroughly for any contamination or defects. In large part that is true, but fresh vegetables, baby food, and human medicines have all been found to be tainted or adulterated, and products for our companion animals are no different. Globalization has brought multiple chains of production and manufacture, which complicate the process and can lead to product defects in dog toys, leashes, beds, food, medicines, and other related products.

Case in Point

The largest recall of pet food in history occurred in 2007.[16] Menu Foods, a Canadian company founded in 1971, discovered that its pet food had

16. MARION NESTLE, PET FOOD POLITICS: THE CHIHUAHUA IN THE COAL MINE (Univ. of California Press 2008).

been contaminated with melamine, an industrial chemical that can be made into hard plastic dinnerware,[17] and cyanuric acid, a by-product of melamine.[18] Cyanuric acid is used to stabilize solutions for chlorinating swimming pools and hot tubs.[19] In Menu Foods' pet food it caused crystals to be formed in the kidneys of dogs and cats, resulting in kidney failure and often death. The food had been adulterated in China, where it was manufactured.

Numerous lawsuits were filed, and in 2008, a U.S. judicial panel consolidated 120 class-action lawsuits and assigned the case to the U.S. district judge in Camden, New Jersey.[20] Menu Foods settled in May 2008 for $24 million.[21]

Menu Foods is not the only pet food manufacturer to recall its products, but it was the largest at the time. The lawsuit was a class-action suit with numerous plaintiffs. There are also individual cases of toys or treats injuring dogs or making them sick. Any claim will need sufficient evidence to prove that the toy or treat caused the problem. Look to the consumer protection laws in your state and seek the advice of a lawyer for guidance on a course of action.

For Owners: Follow recalls and warnings on dog food and product websites. If your dog becomes ill after eating or playing with a toy, contact your veterinarian. Many times there can be more than one possible reason. If you do believe that the food or treat has harmed your dog, contact your veterinarian about conducting any tests necessary to confirm your suspicions.

Police Shootings

Police shoot dogs. Some dogs are killed out of necessity. A dog may have been severely injured in a car accident and a police officer will quickly end the dog's suffering. A dog may be attacking and pose an immediate threat to the life of the police officer or another person. However, the sad truth is

17. *Id.* at 69.
18. *Id.* at 83.
19. *Id.* at 83.
20. *Id.* at 162.
21. *Id.* at 41.

that on many occasions, a beloved family dog is killed needlessly due to a lack of police officer training, failure to plan ahead, mistakes, or indifference on the part of law enforcement.

Case in Point

In 2008, a SWAT team raided the home of Cheye Calvo, the mayor of Berwyn Heights in Prince George County, Maryland, shooting and killing his two Labrador retrievers. Calvo's wife, who is a finance officer for the state, was sent a package that contained marijuana, which the Calvos knew nothing about. According to Calvo, "My government blew through my doors and killed my dogs."[22] Calvo and his mother-in-law were handcuffed and interrogated for hours, surrounded by the dogs' carcasses and pools of the dogs' blood. Prince George County settled a lawsuit by Calvo, the amount of which was not disclosed.[23]

The legal authority that grants law enforcement the power to shoot and kill dogs arises from the government's police power. Unlike acts by private individuals or other entities, the death of a dog at the hands of the police is an act of the government and falls under the category of state action. State action that interferes with our rights to privacy and property invokes the protection of the U.S. Constitution and must be reasonable and legally justified.

Through their police power, states have broad authority to enact laws and exercise control over the actions of individual citizens in order to promote public order and peace and to provide for the general welfare. The concept of police power is not static; it has been evolving throughout history, subject to the needs and wants of society. We constantly balance our rights as individuals against the needs of society and the common good.

---

22. Aaron C. Davis, *Police Raid Berwyn Heights Mayor's Home, Kill His 2 Dogs*, WASH. POST, July 31, 2008, www.washingtonpost.com/wp-dyn/content/article/2008/07/30/AR2008073003299.html (last visited Sept. 6, 2014).
23. *Id.*

Case in Point

In 1876, the U.S. Supreme Court stated:

> When one becomes a member of society, he necessarily parts with some rights or privileges which, as an individual not affected by his relations to others, he might retain."[24]

The acts of other government entities, such as city shelters and animal control agencies, are also considered state action. Courts have long settled that the police power includes the power to regulate various aspects of dog ownership. However, this power is not absolute. Actions must be consistent with our rights under the U.S. Constitution, the laws of the state, and public policy, and they must be employed in a "reasonable" manner. The government cannot unreasonably infringe on individual liberties or property, which is the basis for challenging police shootings.

Lawsuits involving a state actor, such as the police, may be filed under a variety of constitutional theories. State action related to dog issues may involve a violation of rights granted under the Fourteenth Amendment's right to due process clause and the Fourth Amendment's protection against illegal search and seizure. See chapter 2, "The Dog Laws."

These claims are brought under the Civil Rights Act of 1871. The act states:

> Every person who, under color of any statute, ordinance, regulation, custom, or usage, of any State or Territory or the District of Columbia, subjects, or causes to be subjected, any citizen of the United States or other person within the jurisdiction thereof to the deprivation of any rights, privileges, or immunities secured by the Constitution and laws, shall be liable to the party injured in an action at law, suit in equity, or other proper proceeding for redress, except that in any action brought

24. Munn v. Illinois, 94 U.S. 113, 124 (1876).

against a judicial officer for an act or omission taken in such officer's judicial capacity, injunctive relief shall not be granted unless a declaratory decree was violated or declaratory relief was unavailable. For the purposes of this section, any Act of Congress applicable exclusively to the District of Columbia shall be considered to be a statute of the District of Columbia.[25]

Case in Point

In *San Jose Charter of Hells Angels Motorcycle Club v. City of San Jose*, members of the Hells Angels sued the City of San Jose under 42 U.S.C.A. 1983 for a violation of their Fourth Amendment rights.[26] While executing search warrants at the home of two Hells Angels, police officers shot and killed three of the members' dogs. The Court of Appeals for the Ninth Circuit found that the shooting was an unreasonable seizure and an unreasonable execution of the search warrants under the Fourth Amendment. In its discussion of the shooting of the dogs, the court stated, "Reasonableness is the touchstone of any seizure under the Fourth Amendment. . . . Here, the intrusion was severe."[27] The court went on to state that "despite a week to plan for the entry, the officers developed no realistic plan other than shooting the dogs while serving the search warrants."[28]

In these types of cases, the government officials being sued are allowed to assert a defense based on immunity from liability, even though they may have violated the plaintiff's constitutional rights. This is known as the qualified immunity defense. While a government official may claim immunity, the court may not grant it if the defendant's acts were not reasonable.

25. 42 U.S.C. § 1983.
26. San Jose Charter of Hells Angels Motorcycle Club v. City of San Jose, 402 F.3d 962 (9th Cir. 2005).
27. *Id.* at 975.
28. *Id.* at 976.

For Everyone: Constitutional cases are complex and require the expertise of a lawyer, particularly one well versed in constitutional law.

Dangerous Dogs

The issue of dangerous dogs has been consistently at the top of the agenda in many cities and states throughout the country. Dog bites, particularly bites by short-haired muscular mutts alleged to be "pit bulls," have been overreported in the news, making it appear as though there is a national dog-bite epidemic or that there are more dangerous dogs out there than ever before. This perception naturally raises concerns among citizens, and when citizens worry, governments act. As a result, one often sees panic policymaking, which can lead to ineffective legislation, lawsuits, and overreaction surrounding dog bites. However the recent trend at the state level has been to reject breed discrimination. Indeed, 19 states now have provisions prohibiting some form of breed discrimination.

All dogs can bite, and dog-bite situations can happen to anyone. Contrary to what the media publishes or lawmakers pronounce, dog bites transcend breeds, economics, and owners. An even-tempered dog will unexpectedly snap at the child who comes too close to the food bowl. A dog may bite an experienced handler or a gentle owner—virtually all dogs have the potential to bite and will bite under certain circumstances. A recent study of dog-related fatalities revealed that most of the factors involved were in the control of the dogs' owners.[29]

While the law may distinguish between a serious and nonserious injury, both scenarios have the same potential result under the law—the killing of the dog. *For this reason, owners must never assume that a simple explanation will save their dog from being euthanized. If your dog bites a person or a domestic animal, seek the advice of an experienced lawyer because your dog's life is at stake in any dog-bite situation.*

29. Dr. Ken Tudor, *Dog Bite Fatalities: Breed or Human Problem?* PetMD, Daily Vet (Apr. 3, 2013), http://www.petmd.com/blogs/thedailyvet/ken-tudor/2014/april/dog-bite-fatalities-breed-or-human-problem-31529.

Perception or Reality

Is there really a dog-bite epidemic? Are some breeds of dogs inherently dangerous? A closer look at the dog-bite "epidemic" and the "inherently dangerous" breeds reveals more perception, and misperception, than reality.

Despite the media hype, the frequency of dog bites and which breeds bite is much more nuanced. Serious injuries from dog bites are relatively rare and no single breed is responsible.[30]

Dog ownership is on the rise, with approximately 83 million dogs in the United States.[31] That is a significant number of households with dogs. In contrast, statistics comparing the 1970s to 2011 show that dog bites have gone down, drastically in some instances.[32] In Los Angeles County, there were 40,000 reports in 1972, compared to 8,365 in 2011.[33] New York City saw more than a ten-fold decrease over a 40-year period, from 37,488 to 3,557.[34] In Washington, D.C., 5 percent (ten reported dog bites) of all reported bites were categorized as severe.[35] That is ten bites in a city of more than 600,000 people and roughly 280,000 dogs, based on statistics. Further, nine different breeds of dogs were responsible for the ten severe bites.[36]

It is impossible to look at a breed in isolation and obtain an accurate picture. Numerous factors are at play in a dog-bite situation. As far as breeds are concerned, popularity and prevalence are relevant. For example, in some areas of Canada, more fatal dog attacks are attributed to sled dogs and Siberian Huskies, most likely because those breeds are more prevalent.[37] Small breeds may be less likely to cause harm, and incidents may not be reported. A number of humane organizations have promoted the policy that "dangerous and/or vicious animals should be labeled as such

30. *See generally* NATIONAL CANINE RESEARCH COUNCIL, www.nationalcanineresearchcouncil.com (last visited Sept. 6, 2014).
31. Pets by the Numbers, HSUS, at http://www.humanesociety.org/issues/pet_overpopulation/facts/pet_ownership_statistics.html (last visited September 2014).
32. NATIONAL CANINE RESEARCH COUNCIL, www.nationalcanineresearchcouncil.com/dogbites/reported-bites-decreasing (last visited Sept. 6, 2014).
33. *Id.*
34. *Id.*
35. *Id.*
36. *Id.*
37. AVMA, *The Role of Breed in Dog Bite Risk and Prevention*, https://www.avma.org/KB/Resources/LiteratureReviews/Pages/The-Role-of-Breed-in-Dog-Bite-Risk-and-Prevention.aspx (last visited Sept. 6, 2014).

as a result of their actions or behavior and not because of their breed." Another report notes that "[t]here is no scientific evidence that one kind of dog is more likely to bite or injure a human being than another kind."[38] On August 19, 2013, the White House issued a statement that the Obama administration does not support breed-specific legislation, citing the position taken by the Centers for Disease Control research showing that bans are largely ineffective and a waste of public resources.[39] The American Bar Association passed a resolution calling for the enactment of comprehensive breed-neutral dangerous-dog and reckless owner laws and the repeal of all breed-discriminatory or breed-specific provisions.[40]

So if it is not breed-related, why do dogs bite? One of the determining factors in dog bites is whether or not the dog has been sterilized. Intact dogs bite more frequently than sterilized dogs.[41] Socialization and supervision are important. Isolated dogs and those who are chained and tethered may be fearful, and fearful dogs will bite. Those who are chained or tethered cannot flee, increasing their fear if someone approaches.[42] Dogs who have been abused have reason to fear humans and may be more aggressive. And provocation is a factor. Dogs that are in pain, being harmed, protecting food or territory, or nursing offspring are in situations where they are more likely to bite. Children are at greater risk because they may make loud noises or run toward the dog, creating fear. All of these factors point to one main cause—how we humans treat dogs.

The Law

The first treatise on the law relating to dogs was published in the 19th century. London lawyer and author Fredrick Lupton considered the subject of

38. Cynthia Bathurst, Donald Cleary, Karen Delise, Ledy VanKavage & Patricia Rushing, *The Problem of Dog-Related Incident and Encounters,* COPS 9 (August 2011), www.dogwise.com/downloader.cfm?itemid=dogincidents&format=pdf.

39. NATIONAL CANINE RESEARCH COUNCIL, http://www.nationalcanineresearchcouncil.com/blog/obama-administration-opposes-breed-specific-legislation-bsl (last visited Sept. 6, 2014).

40. AM. BAR ASS'N, http://www.americanbar.org/content/dam/aba/administrative/mental_physical_disability/Resolution_100.authcheckdam.pdf (last visited Sept. 6, 2014).

41. Bathurst et al., *supra* note 38, at 9.

42. *Id.*

dogs and the law to be "a subject of no slight importance."[43] The treatise devotes two chapters to injuries caused by dogs and sets out four canine classifications: "(1) ferocious; (2) dangerous; (3) mischievous; and (4) harmless."[44] Although Lupton saw little difference among the first three, the definitions did vary somewhat. A ferocious dog was defined as "one of naturally savage disposition, of which he has already given proof by attacking or biting men and animals."[45] A mischievous dog was one with a tendency to jump on people and chase livestock.[46]

Fast-forward more than 100 years and we find that dog laws and the dangerous dog are still "of no slight importance" in our legal system, and the terms "ferocious" and "mischievous" have been generally replaced by descriptions such as "vicious" and "aggressive." However, there is a major difference between the companions from Lupton's time, which were presumed to be of a "tame and gentle disposition"[47] by nature, and today's perception by some that certain breeds are inherently dangerous. An inherently dangerous nature places dogs in the same category as tigers and other wild animals.

Dog Bites

Lupton's dog-bite laws were part of England's common law, handed down through court decisions over time. Today, many states and cities have codified their laws covering dangerous dogs and have statutes, although the provisions vary, making it difficult to make too many generalizations. There are laws covering dog bites to humans and some state laws include dog bites and harm to other domestic animals.

Below are some of the provisions and exceptions that may be found in various dog-bite laws. Check the laws in your state and city.

- A bite may be categorized based on severity, such as whether or not the injury was serious. A serious injury is one "characterized by severe

43. FREDRICK LUPTON, THE LAW RELATING TO DOGS, LEGAL TREATISES, 1800–1926 (BiblioLife Network, authentic repro. 1898).
44. *Id.* at ch. 1
45. *Id.*
46. *Id.*
47. *Id* at 4.

bite wounds . . . that would cause a reasonably prudent person to seek treatment from a medical professional and would require hospitalization" or one that results in the death of the victim.[48]

- Some statutes elevate the crime and/or punishment of the owner if the dog has a previous history of bites.
- The law may specifically address a bite to a child or elderly victim.
- A dog's behavior may be excused if provoked. Dogs who are injured and in pain, are being abused or tortured, are protecting offspring or food, and are protecting another person are circumstances that may be included in dog-bite statutes.
- Circumstances, such as whether the person bitten was trespassing on private property, can be a factor.
- If the dog was a police dog used in law enforcement, that will be taken into account.
- Laws may prevent recidivist bad dog owners from owning dogs for a period of time.
- Laws may prevent convicted felons from owning or residing with unsterilized dogs for a number of years after incarceration.

Prevention

Before you think about what to do if your dog bites someone, think about what to do to prevent your dog from biting. Consider the temperament of the dog you have now and the steps you can take to create a safe environment for you, your dog, and those who come into contact with her. Shelter and rescue dogs may have no known history, so use caution, particularly around children. Train your dog and learn about dog behavior and why dogs may bite. Spay or neuter your dog. Know that certain types of play with your dog may seem innocent but could be training your dog to be aggressive. Chaining or tethering a dog is a known cause of aggression. When you are out with your dog, maintain control at all times. Be extra vigilant around children when out. Their sudden movements and loud noises can frighten even the gentlest of dogs. Teach your own children how to properly approach and pet a dog. Check with your insurer

48. TEX. HEALTH & SAFETY CODE § 822.001 (2).

to make sure you are covered in the event your dog bites, at home or in another location.

If Your Dog Bites

If your dog bites someone, the outcome will depend on the state and local laws where the incident occurred, the people involved, the dog involved, and the circumstances. The possible scenarios surrounding dog bites are countless, making it impractical to cover even a few scenarios. What follows is a basic overview of a dangerous-dog case, laws and ordinances that may apply, and possible outcomes.

First, if it is a serious bite, call 911 or get the person to a hospital immediately. Secure your dog in a safe place. Then seek the advice of an experienced animal law lawyer who has handled dog-bite cases. This is a serious legal and safety issue, and it is not one that can be addressed in this book.

Fortunately for dogs and humans, most bites do not cause serious injuries. Less than 2 percent of individuals visiting an emergency room for a dog bite require hospitalization.[49] So chances are that the bite inflicted by your dog is not serious. Although it may not be serious, the act of being bitten by a dog is stressful nonetheless, particularly if you have a big dog or if the incident involves a young or elderly person. Take the time to make sure the person is all right, then think of the situation as you would a car accident—look for witnesses and get statements and witness contact information, take photos, exchange contact information with the person bitten, and discuss the circumstances with the person, if possible. Try to determine why your dog may have bitten, and whether she may have been provoked. If you think the person might have provoked your dog, try to find surveillance evidence through cameras. Many urban neighborhoods have blue light cameras, but you must obtain the footage quickly or it will be deleted. A lawyer can help you obtain it.

Finally, immediately retain a lawyer who is experienced in defending dog-bite cases. If there is no experienced lawyer in your area, the lawyer you retain should seek the advice of one in your state who can guide your lawyer through the process. Listed below are the general steps that follow a dog bite.

---

49. Bathurst et al., *supra* note 38, at 7.

The Process

If your dog bites someone, and it is reported, two legal actions may follow. The first action is by the city or county where the bite occurred. Municipalities are charged with protecting their citizens, and animal control is one of those responsibilities. The city's investigation and hearing, if there is one, will determine whether or not your dog should be declared dangerous under the law, and if so, what steps should be taken to ensure that your dog does not bite again. Here are the general steps that are taken:

- A report is filed. It may be a sworn affidavit from the person bitten.
- Animal control, the sheriff, or the police will show up to investigate. Even if the bite was not serious, an investigation is warranted to ensure that the dog has been vaccinated for rabies. If the person goes to the doctor or hospital, health-care workers are likely required to report the bite regardless of what the victim wants. Even if it is a minor injury, it is nonetheless a dog bite in the eyes of the law.
- It is more than likely that animal control will want to take your dog and quarantine him to ensure that he does not have rabies, regardless of whether you have proof of vaccinations. If possible, and a lawyer can advise you, try to get permission to quarantine your dog at home or at your vet's office. Quarantine can be stressful, and ten days can turn into ten weeks or more if you find yourself in a protracted legal battle. You do not want to give up possession of your dog if you can avoid it.
- A hearing will be held. This is where many dog owners take their first misstep by assuming they do not need legal representation. Think about it. Prosecutors and judges have little to lose in finding a dog dangerous, but they have much to lose if they free your dog and she bites someone else.
- If your dog is declared dangerous, there is usually an appeals process. Sadly, your dog may have to stay in quarantine while the appeal is completed.

In the best-case scenario, the bite was not serious, the person injured does not wish to pursue it, and the city gives you nothing more than a warning. A less desirable scenario is that your dog is declared dangerous but is not euthanized. In this situation, you will be have to comply with any number of dangerous-dog requirements that have been established, such as:

- A yearly registration fee, which can range from $50 to more than $500 a year.
- Mandatory liability insurance. In Texas, the required amount is $100,000. The challenge may not be the cost of insurance but finding a carrier willing to insure.
- A stronger enclosure or fence.
- Sterilization and microchipping.
- Special collars, harnesses, or identification. Dogs may be required to be muzzled in public.
- Exterior signs on homes or apartments, indicating that a dangerous dog is located in the home.

While the above restrictions can be onerous, what is worse is that some jurisdictions require that the dog be removed from the jurisdiction if found to be dangerous. It means your dog can live, but you will have to find another home for your dog if you cannot leave as well. Some cities are refusing to take dogs that have been declared dangerous, so finding another home for your dog may be more difficult than you think. What the city cannot do is maintain its legal authority over your dog once you remove him from the jurisdiction.

Case in Point

I received a call from a dog owner whose dog had been declared dangerous. The sheriff indicated that the owner was to continue to report the dog's whereabouts once the dog left the jurisdiction. The law stated that the dog was to leave the jurisdiction. The owner was required to prove that the dog had left the jurisdiction, but she was not required to continue to report the dog's location once out of the jurisdiction.

In the worst-case scenario, the person injured does push the issue and wants your dog euthanized; or the city's public policy is zero tolerance, and it pursues every dog bite to the fullest extent and wants to euthanize your dog.

Or, your dog may be dangerous beyond rehabilitation, given the dog's past history and mistreatment. If your dog is to be euthanized, your right to an appeal, and the type of appeal, may be limited, and you will definitely need the assistance of a lawyer.

The second legal suit that may occur in the event of a dog bite is a civil lawsuit for money damages filed against you personally for the injury to the person bitten. The person will hire a lawyer and file suit against you personally for damages. If you have homeowners or renters insurance, you simply turn it over to your insurance company to handle. These cases are about money damages, so there is no risk that your dog will be euthanized or banished from the city. The insurance company will decide whether to defend in court or to settle out of court. If you do not have insurance, you will have to personally defend yourself in court. In some cases, the defendant will declare bankruptcy in order to avoid paying damages.

Chapter 5

ANIMAL CRUELTY AND THE LAW

Do dogs feel pain? Do they suffer? For most of us, the answer is a clear and emphatic yes. We see it when our dogs are injured and in the heartbreaking cases of animal abuse covered in the news. Surprisingly, the view that dogs and other animals feel pain was not always considered true, and such views have continued to influence our perceptions of animals.

Case in Point

Dogs as machines? René Descartes was a 17th-century philosopher who set forth the idea that animals were "automata," simply machines without minds, souls, or the ability to feel pain.[1] He argued that because animals had no consciousness and no language, they had no feelings. Descartes and his followers, the Cartesians, experimented on live dogs and cats, dissecting them without anesthesia. Descartes claimed that the animals' cries and screams were merely the noise of machinery breaking.[2]

1. For a discussion of Descartes, *see* Bernard E. Rollin, The Unheeded Cry: Animal Consciousness, Animal Pain, and Science 24 (Iowa State Univ. Press expanded ed. 1998).
2. *See* Andrew Linzey, Why Animal Suffering Matters: Philosophy, Theology, and Practical Ethics 45 (Oxford Univ. Press 2009).

While Descartes' view of dogs as machines seems strange today, he was an influential philosopher and his views carried weight and served various purposes at the time. Bernard Rollin, a contemporary philosopher, suggests that Descartes' view was appealing in that it eased the minds of the researchers who, at the time, were forced to do invasive research on animals without anesthesia.[3] Since they believed animals felt no pain, they could believe animal cruelty did not exist, and thus no issues of ethics or morality were raised in their treatment of animals.

Of course there was no shortage of philosophers and religious leaders willing to challenge Descartes on his views of animal sentience and suffering, but it was Henry Bergh, a 19th-century New York aristocrat and humanitarian, who moved the ills of animal cruelty to the forefront. The founder of the American Society for the Prevention of Cruelty to Animals, Bergh was a tireless crusader and exposed cruelty against horses that pulled carriages, the mistreatment of livestock, pigeon shoots, vivisection, and dog fighting.[4] He lobbied for anticruelty laws, and his philosophy of protecting animals "was an issue that crossed party lines and class boundaries."[5] His wealth and standing in society meant that he had the ear of a broad audience that included powerful businessmen and government leaders. His argument was basic, that "[animal abuse] is a matter purely of conscience; it has no perplexing side issues. It is a moral question in all its aspects."[6] Bergh used his power and influence to pass legislation, fight animal cruelty on the streets, and communicate his message that cruelty in any form is morally unacceptable. There have been many crusaders since Bergh, but his work served to accelerate the animal protection movement and has left a lasting imprint on the law.

Animal Abuse and Human Violence

Concurrent with Bergh's message that animal cruelty is morally wrong in and of itself was the belief that animal abuse was an indication of an immoral person, one who would find it easy to harm humans. However,

3. ROLLIN, *supra* note 1, at 24.
4. ASPCA, http://www.aspca.org/about-us/about-the-aspca/history-aspca (last visited Sept. 6, 2014).
5. *Id.*
6. *Id.*

there was no empirical evidence at the time to support this view. It was based on society's moral compass, a logical conclusion that a person who took pleasure in causing the suffering of animals was only one step away from taking pleasure in causing the suffering of humans.

Today, the link between animal abuse and human violence is based on more than logic. Much research has been conducted that shows that certain markers, including animal cruelty, will make an individual more likely to engage in human violence.[7] The Federal Bureau of Investigation "believes that animal abuse is not a harmless venting of emotion by a healthy individual."[8] Serial killers such as Ted Bundy, David Berkowitz ("Son of Sam"), Albert DeSalvo (the "Boston Strangler"), and Jeffrey Dahmer all committed incidents of animal cruelty in their childhoods.[9]

Because of its concern with the link between animal abuse and the early identification of violent criminals, the National Sheriff's Association began advocating for greater training and resources for law enforcement and the collection of animal cruelty data in the Uniform Crime Report and Incident Based Reporting System (NIBRS).[10] In September 2014, FBI Director James Comey approved the Advisory Board Policy's recommendation to include animal cruelty in the NIBRS.[11] The connection between animal cruelty and human violence continues to be debated, but the FBI and the National Sheriff's Association have clearly stated their position.

One situation where animal abuse and human violence intersect is in domestic violence. Abusers harm family pets in order to hurt the victim. In many instances, the victim will not leave home because she cannot take the animal. Assistance in these situations requires strategies such as cross-reporting on the part of social services, law enforcement, and animal welfare organizations; pet-friendly shelters; animals in protective orders; and special laws. In Indiana, there is a separate statute called Domestic Violence Animal Cruelty, a Class D felony, defined as a "person who knowingly or

---

7. *See* CHILD ABUSE, DOMESTIC VIOLENCE, AND ANIMAL ABUSE: LINKING THE CIRCLES OF COMPASSION FOR PREVENTION AND INTERVENTION (Frank Ascione & Phil Arkow eds., 1999).
8. *Id.* at 34.
9. *Id.* at 105.
10. National Sheriff's Association Advocates for the Addition of Animal Cruelty to the UCR and NIBRS, at https://www.sheriffs.org/sites/default/files/uploads/documents/GovAffairs/2013-02%20Animal%20Cruelty.pdf (last visited Sept. 22, 2014).
11. *See* the Animal Legal Defense Fund, at http://aldf.org/blog/tracking-animal-crimes-data-in-the-fbis-uniform-crime-reporting-ucr-program-a-huge-step-forward (last visited Sept. 22, 2014).

intentionally kills a vertebrate animal with the intent to threaten, intimidate, coerce, harass, or terrorize a family or household member."[12]

The Law

Today, animal cruelty, with various exceptions, is a crime and can constitute a felony in every state. Most cruelty laws are found at the state and local levels and may be investigated and enforced by animal control officers, law enforcement, or humane organizations in some jurisdictions. Animal cruelty may be categorized as a misdemeanor or the more serious felony. The classification will depend on various factors, including the perpetrator's criminal intent (referred to as "mens rea"), the severity of the act, and the overall facts and circumstances.

Any animal may be a victim of cruelty, and it occurs in many settings—in breeding, agriculture, scientific research, domestic violence, and animal fighting. The laws are inconsistent, and what constitutes animal cruelty against one animal may not be a crime against another, or it may be viewed differently under different circumstances. Some laws address cruelty against companion animals or livestock while exempting others. Certain activities, such as hunting, are usually exempted under the law.

Acts of cruelty against dogs include felony acts, such as intentionally setting a dog on fire, as well as acts of negligence, such as failing to provide adequate food and water. Cruelty is found in domestic violence situations, where the abuser uses cruelty against the family dog to hurt the victim, as well as in hoarding cases, where the owner believes she is actually helping the animals, contrary to the reality of the situation.

Punishment

Convictions for animal cruelty can result in a range of punishments, the types and lengths of which vary by state. Convictions may involve probation, jail time, and/or a fine. In general, abuse by a repeat offender, abuse with a deadly weapon, or abuse with the intent to cause harm to a person

12. IND. CODE § 35-46-3-12.5 (2014).

can enhance the sentence, resulting in ten or more years in jail. Other types of punishment may focus more on rehabilitation, such as community service, counseling, or cruelty education programs. A convicted offender will certainly lose possession of his dog if the dog has survived the cruelty, and he may be prohibited from owning another dog permanently or for an extended period of time. If the dog has been held in a city shelter or humane organization, or if the perpetrator has abused another person's dog, she may be required to pay restitution in replacement, veterinary, and housing costs. Further, cruelty to an assistance animal may mandate enhanced punishment.

As you can see, animal cruelty is far from simple, legally or socially. Different acts, mental states, and actors result in a complex set of laws. And numerous legal exemptions and defenses apply.

Mens Rea (Culpability)

Criminal law is centered on the concept that there is a mental state in the commission of a crime and a physical act. The mental state is defined under the Latin term mens rea, meaning "guilty mind." Terms such as "intentionally," "negligently," "maliciously," "knowingly," and "recklessly" are used in the law to describe various mental states to be considered in assessing the severity of the crime. The man who "maliciously" and repeatedly beats his dog with a baseball bat and does this with the intent to torture the dog will evoke little sympathy from society and the courts.[13] The 83-year-old widow who takes in homeless dogs to help them but becomes unable physically and financially to care for them will be viewed differently based on her mental state.[14]

The Physical Act

The other element in the crime of animal cruelty is the physical act itself. It may be described in various ways. A felony act of animal cruelty in Texas includes torture, with torture defined as an act that causes "unjustifiable pain and suffering."[15] Other acts include one who "kills,

13. *See* People v. Bunt, 462 N.Y.S.2d 142 (N.Y. Just. Ct. 1983).
14. *See* Martinez v. State of Texas, 48 S.W.3d 273 (Tex. Ct. App.—San Antonio 2001). Note the conflicts of the judges.
15. Tex. Penal Code Ann. § 42.092 (a)(8) (2013).

administers poison to, or causes serious bodily injury."[16] Aggravated cruelty is a felony in Colorado and includes knowingly torturing, needlessly mutilating, or needlessly killing an animal.[17] And in Hawaii, a felony act of cruelty is one that involves "ten or more pet animals in any one instance."[18]

Acts of animal cruelty that do not rise to the level of a felony are usually classified as misdemeanors. Misdemeanor cruelty typically involves physical acts of neglect and abandonment, such as a person who "recklessly, knowingly, or intentionally abandons or neglects the animal."[19]

Negligent Cruelty

As you learned in chapter 3, "The Legal Basics of Dog Ownership," owners in most states are legally required to provide adequate care for their dogs. There are of course disagreements regarding what defines adequate care, but at a minimum it means nutritious food, clean water, and shelter that provides protection from the elements. The failure to provide minimal care may be negligent cruelty, which can be a result of indifference and insensitivity to the needs of a living, sentient creature; or, it may be the result of a lack of education and awareness of what is required for the health and safety of a dog. It may also be economic. A family may have incurred a financial hardship and be unable to adequately provide for their dog. Situations of negligence require accurate assessments by investigators and the creation of solutions that match the problem, whether it is prosecution, education, community support, financial help, or the voluntary surrender of the dog.

Case in Point

A female dog who had just given birth to puppies was found roaming the streets and appeared to be starving. Animal control investigated

16. *Id.* § 42.092 (b)(2) (2013).
17. COLO. REV. STAT. ANN. § 18-9-202 (1.5)(b) (2014).
18. HAW. REV. STAT. § 711-1109(4) (2014).
19. IND. CODE § 35-46-3-7 (a)(2) (2014).

and learned that the dog's family did not have the funds to repair their fence where the dog had escaped. They were feeding their dog but did not understand why the dog was so thin. Rather than seize the dog, animal control provided the family with basic education on dog ownership and low-cost veterinary care, and it alerted a humane organization that voluntarily repairs fences. Animal control had the dog spayed to prevent any future litters of puppies and made regular visits to the family to check on the dog. Several months later the dog was healthy and the family members were found to be responsible dog owners.

Felony Cruelty

All animal cruelty is serious. The intent behind cruelty that is classified as negligent is not always clear and may be related to apathy, psychological problems, or money, or it may be a result of a lack of education or resources. However, felony animal cruelty goes beyond negligence. It is malicious and done with the specific purpose of causing a dog, and at times a person, to suffer. Dangerous weapons such as knives, fire, or guns may be used. Cruelty such as dog fighting may also involve gambling, illegal guns, or other crimes. Because of the seriousness of these crimes, they are classified as state felonies or federal crimes with enhanced punishments.

Case in Point

In 2012, four young men in Dallas, Texas, were convicted of felony animal cruelty for killing a mixed-breed puppy by pouring lighter fluid on him and setting him on fire. The puppy was tortured for entertainment, with witnesses stating that the perpetrators were laughing as the puppy ran, crying in pain. Efforts to save the puppy failed, and he died a few days later. The ringleader in the case received a five-year jail sentence because a deadly weapon, fire, was used in the abuse.

The Many Faces of Animal Cruelty

Hoarding

It is difficult to speak of animal cruelty in generalities with a one-size-fits-all approach to stopping it. Acts of cruelty have the same impact on a dog—unnecessary suffering, injury, or death—but may be inflicted unintentionally or unknowingly and seemingly with good intent. Animal hoarders fit into this latter group and constitute an unusual and difficult situation of animal cruelty.

Hoarding in general is a compulsion to collect items to an excessive degree, with the inability to get rid of them. Animal hoarding is the compulsion to collect animals. The Hoarding Animals Research Consortium (HARC) states: "The pathological accumulation of animals was first described in 1981 and animal hoarding was formally defined in the public health literature in 1999 using the following criteria:

- Having more than the typical number of companion animals.
- Failing to provide even minimal standards of nutrition, sanitation, shelter, and veterinary care, with this neglect often resulting in illness and death from starvation, spread of infectious disease, and untreated injury or medical condition.
- Denial of the inability to provide this minimum care and the impact of that failure on the animals, the household, and human occupants of the dwelling.
- Persistence, despite this failure, in accumulating and controlling animals."[20]

The hoarder's denial of her inability to care for the animals results in unnecessary suffering and death. Animal hoarders often claim that they are saving animals by taking them in, despite their obvious inability to care for them. According to the HARC, the answer to hoarding is intervention

20. HOARDING OF ANIMALS RESEARCH CONSORTIUM (HARC), http://vet.tufts.edu/hoarding/abthoard.htm#A1 (last visited Sept. 6, 2014).

and treatment, not prosecution for animal cruelty. Without help, the recidivism rate of hoarders is close to 100 percent.[21]

Most states have yet to comprehensively address the unique issues related to animal hoarding. Hoarders are ordinarily prosecuted under the general animal cruelty statutes. Two states, Hawaii and Illinois, have specific laws related to animal hoarding.

Case in Point

The Illinois law is known as the Companion Animal Hoarder Act. A hoarder is defined as "a person who (i) possesses a large number of companion animals; (ii) fails to or is unable to provide what he or she is required to provide under Section 3 of this Act; (iii) keeps the companion animals in a severely overcrowded environment; and (iv) displays an inability to recognize or understand the nature of or has a reckless disregard for the conditions under which the companion animals are living and the deleterious impact they have on the companion animals' and owner's health and well-being."[22]

An important provision in the law requires a person convicted of hoarding to obtain treatment:

> If the convicted person is a juvenile or a companion animal hoarder, the court must order the convicted person to undergo a psychological or psychiatric evaluation and to undergo treatment that the court determines to be appropriate after due consideration of the evaluation.[23]

Animal hoarding is receiving greater attention for the damage to both the person and the animals. Expect more laws to be passed like the Illinois law, which appropriately addresses the act and the mental state.

21. *Id.*
22. 510 ILL. COMP. STAT. § 70/2.10 (2014).
23. *Id.* § 70/3(d) (2014).

Overextended Rescue Groups

Rescue groups have proliferated at a fast pace. All breeds, as well as different combinations of breeds, are represented and they are found in foster homes and shelter facilities across the country. Rescue groups have saved the lives of countless dogs, and volunteers give selflessly of their time and money. They often operate on shoestring budgets and use their own personal funds.

The laws governing rescue groups vary by state. Their treatment of the dogs they rescue usually falls under the general animal cruelty and health laws in the states where they operate. They may also have to comply with the general laws related to operating a business or nonprofit, or they may be required to comply with specific laws related to the operation of the rescue.

Case in Point

Oregon has record-keeping and licensing requirements if a rescue group accepts donations and keeps ten or more animals.

> (2)(a) Maintain a record for each animal. . . .
> (2)(b) Permit an authorized representative of the enforcing agency to inspect records. . . .
> (3)(a) The entity shall obtain a license issued by the enforcing agency.[24]

Unfortunately, some rescue groups unwittingly cross the line when they become unable, financially and/or physically, to care for the number of dogs in their care but continue to take in more dogs. Unlike hoarding, rescue groups simply overextend themselves in an effort to save as many dogs as possible, an admirable, but sometimes impossible, goal. Rescue groups depend on volunteers and contributions, and if either is lacking, dogs may

24. OR. REV. STAT. § 609.415 (2013).

suffer from neglect due to lack of veterinary care, exercise, or proper nutrition. Additionally, the physical space may become overcrowded, causing the dogs to spread illness and disease. As with hoarding, solutions may lie not in animal cruelty prosecutions but in community assistance and support.

Puppy Mills

The horrors of puppy mills have been a topic in the media and in state legislatures across the country, as well as at the federal level of government. "Puppy mill" is a term used to describe large-scale commercial breeding operations whose motivation is pure profit, with little or no concern for animal welfare except as it benefits the business. The scenes from puppy mill raids are tragic and disheartening. Dogs spend their entire lives in wire cages stacked upon each other where feces and urine fall down to those at the bottom; the dogs receive little to no veterinary care; females are bred repeatedly and never given a rest; and the dogs do not receive adequate exercise or fresh air. Dogs rescued from puppy mills may have never felt the earth beneath their feet or breathed fresh air. They are merely commodities, given as little care and attention as possible. This is one form of animal cruelty at its worst—abuse due to apathy and indifference by commercial breeders who place no value on a dog's life except for the income generated from the puppies.

Nationally, the USDA's Animal Welfare Act governs commercial breeders, but exposés and raids of facilities have shown that despite efforts, enforcement is largely ineffective and federal resources are insufficient to address the widespread problems. Breeders are given repeated warnings and citations but often continue business as usual, even when fined. Due to greater exposure of the inhumane practices associated with puppy mills, some states have enacted their own laws in an effort to impose greater accountability on breeders and to stop blatant cruelty. The laws vary widely, but generally they provide for a permitting system that sets minimum standards for housing and care, allows regular inspections, and establishes fines and various punishments for violations.

What constitutes a commercial breeder varies by state, but it usually includes the number of intact dogs owned and sales activity. In West Virginia, a commercial breeder is any person who "[m]aintains eleven or more unsterilized dogs over the age of one year for the exclusive purpose of actively breeding and is engaged in the business of breeding dogs as household pets for direct or indirect sale or for exchange in return for consideration."[25] Laws also exempt certain groups and dogs, such as those raised for herding, hunting, or greyhound racing.

The strongest laws will address the following:

- Adequate housing, such as sanitary conditions, ventilation, stability, protection from extreme temperatures, solid floors, and the elimination of stacked enclosures.
- Proper veterinary care, including certification of vaccinations and health certification for breeding females. A level of veterinary care for the dogs is mandated, as some breeders opt to treat their own dogs for illnesses and problems without a veterinarian.
- Minimum amounts of exercise and fresh air. Puppy mill dogs may spend their entire lives indoors.
- Protection for potential purchasers, such as veterinarian health certificates, display of current permits, and advertising requirements.
- Consumer remedies for sick and diseased puppies. Breeders may offer a new puppy without reimbursement for veterinary expenses. An exchange of puppies may also mean that the sick puppy is not treated but is euthanized, which is unacceptable to many purchasers. This issue may be addressed in a puppy mill law or a puppy lemon law, similar to lemon laws for cars.
- Regular inspections, including responses to reports by trained law enforcement or humane investigators.
- An anonymous reporting scheme for anyone who believes a facility is in violation of the law.
- Fines and criminal penalties that compel compliance, and provisions allowing the seizure of the animals and/or the closing of the facility for egregious or repeated violations until corrected. Small fines may

25. W. VA. CODE ANN. § 19-20-26 (West 2014).

be ineffective when the breeder weighs the fine against the financial benefit of continuing to violate the law.

- Regular criminal background checks. Anyone convicted of animal cruelty is denied a permit.
- Effective enforcement and follow-up.

These laws are a step in the right direction, but they are only as good as the enforcement behind them.

Reporting, Investigations, and Prosecutions

In order to encourage reporting and investigations of animal cruelty, local governments have systems that allow anonymous reports. However, keep in mind that this makes the job of the prosecutor more difficult. Also, some private and nonprofit organizations have established animal cruelty hotlines in order to raise awareness of animal cruelty and further promote reporting, investigations, and prosecutions.

Case in Point

Animal Protection of New Mexico, a nonprofit animal advocacy organization, has a toll-free hotline for reporting animal cruelty. Information that leads to the arrest and conviction of anyone involved in extreme animal cruelty is eligible for up to $5,000 in reward money.[26]

Veterinarians can play a significant role in investigating and prosecuting animal cruelty. Convictions can turn on the testimony of a veterinarian, and a report of suspected cruelty can prompt an investigation and prosecution. Many people assume that all veterinarians are required to report suspected

26. ANIMAL PROTECTION OF NEW MEXICO, http://apnm.org/campaigns/cruelty/ (last visited Sept. 6, 2014).

cases of animal cruelty, but they are not. However, in some states, such as Oregon, veterinary reporting and investigation are mandated.

Case in Point

Oregon's law states in part:

> The Legislative Assembly finds that there is a direct link between the problems of animal abuse and human abuse and further finds that for the purposes of identifying and prosecuting individuals who have committed crimes against animals, preventing further abuse of animals and preventing animal abuse from escalating to abuse against humans, it is necessary and in the public interest to require mandatory reporting of aggravated animal abuse by veterinarians.[27]

Oregon also mandates investigation by law enforcement:

> (1) A law enforcement agency receiving a report of suspected aggravated animal abuse . . . shall investigate the nature and cause of the suspected aggravated animal abuse.
> (2) If the law enforcement agency finds reasonable cause to believe that aggravated animal abuse has occurred, the law enforcement agency shall process the case in the same manner as any other criminal investigation.[28]

To encourage reporting and protect them from lawsuits, veterinarians are usually given immunity from liability in the event they are mistaken but have reported suspected cruelty in good faith. Illinois goes a step beyond reporting and immunity by requiring veterinarians to cooperate in the investigation.[29]

27. OR. REV. STAT. § 686.442 (2014).
28. OR. REV. STAT. § 686.460 (2014).
29. 510 ILL. COMP. STAT. § 70/3.07 (2014).

Case in Point

Veterinarian Reports

> Any veterinarian in this State who observes or is presented with an animal or animals for the treatment of aggravated cruelty under Section 3.02 or torture under Section 3.03 of this Act must file a report with the Department and cooperate with the Department by furnishing the owner's name, the date of receipt of the animal or animals and any treatment administered, and a description of the animal or animals involved, including a microchip number if applicable. Any veterinarian who in good faith makes a report, as required by this Section, has immunity from any liability, civil, criminal, or otherwise, that may result from his or her actions. For the purposes of any proceedings, civil or criminal, the good faith of the veterinarian shall be presumed.[30]

Generally, humane societies, animal control, law enforcement, and the local sheriff may all conduct animal cruelty investigations at the state and local levels. Even if law enforcement personnel conduct the investigation, they usually need the assistance of humane organizations experienced in animal cruelty investigations and veterinarians who can conduct forensic studies to be used in a prosecution. Some cities have special animal cruelty units trained in the specific issues related to animal cruelty. When a city shows its dedication to prosecuting animal cruelty, an increase in reporting, investigations, and prosecutions will follow.

Case in Point

In Dallas, Texas, the Animal Cruelty Unit is a specialized division of the district attorney's office dedicated to protecting animals from neglect and

Continued

30. *Id.*

Case in Point *Continued*

mistreatment. The district attorney's office recognizes the "need for the effective prosecution of offenders who neglect, torture and kill animals."[31]

There are fewer animal cruelty laws at the federal level than at state and local levels. Those laws that do exist are investigated by the Department of Justice, the Federal Bureau of Investigation, or the enforcement divisions specific to various federal laws. Local or state law enforcement personnel may also collaborate with federal investigators. Dog fighting is one such crime under the federal AWA and can involve gambling, drug dealing, or other federal crimes. One provision of the act makes it a crime to sponsor or exhibit an animal in an animal fighting venture; to buy, sell, deliver, possess, train, or transport animals for participation in an animal fighting venture; or to use the U.S. Postal Service or any other interstate instrumentality to promote or further a fight.[32]

Case in Point

In 2007, Michael Vick, a professional football player, pleaded guilty to conspiracy to travel in interstate commerce in aid of unlawful activities and to sponsor a dog in an animal-fighting venture. He was sentenced to 23 months in prison and was suspended from the National Football League. After his release in July 2009, he was reinstated in the National Football League and signed a contract with the Philadelphia Eagles. The seized dogs were treated and assessed and either went on to happy forever homes or remain in the care of Best Friends Animal Society in Kanab, Utah.[33]

31. Dallas County District Attorney's Office Animal Cruelty Unit, https://www.dallasda.com/division/animal-cruelty-unit (last visited Sept. 6, 2014).
32. 7 U.S.C. § 2156 (2014), *amended by* Pub. L. No. 113-79 (Feb. 7, 2014).
33. This is one of the more interesting cases of dog fighting for a number of reasons—too many to cover adequately in this book. If you are interested in knowing more, several good books have been written about the Vick dogs.

The Process

The prosecution of animal cruelty involves a number of steps and a team of experts. There must be: (1) a report of suspected cruelty; (2) an investigation and the gathering of evidence, including seizure of the dog; (3) an evaluation of the evidence and a decision on whether or not to prosecute; (4) the filing of charges and an arrest; (5) trial preparation/discovery; (6) the entering of the defendant's plea (guilty, not guilty, or no contest); and (7) the trial and/or sentencing (if guilty) or acquittal. If convicted, the defendant may appeal. The law varies by state in designating whether a judge or jury determines the sentence if the defendant is convicted.

Reports of cruelty can come from neighbors, family members, humane organizations, or other witnesses. Once a report is filed, the appropriate entities investigate and make an assessment. Training and experience in animal cruelty cases is vital.

The first step is to assess the situation. It may be a single act of cruelty or a situation where there are multiple acts. If a dog has been killed or severely abused and needs veterinary medical care, investigators will take immediate action to seize the dog. Even in cases of abuse, dogs are still legally the property of their owners, and law enforcement personnel cannot seize a dog without proper legal authority. If the owner is present, they may ask permission to take the dog for veterinary care; or, they may expedite a warrant or be vested with the legal authority to seize the dog. The steps they take depend on the specific laws of the jurisdiction. The investigation and gathering of evidence, particularly in the death of a dog, is a critical element in a successful prosecution. Without a cause of death, it is difficult, if not impossible, to prosecute.

In cases of neglect, where a dog is malnourished or dehydrated or shows other signs of neglect, investigators will talk with the owner and try to determine whether there are educational or financial issues or another reason why the dog is not being properly cared for. Once those issues are determined, investigators will take the steps they deem necessary to help the dog and the owner. Although a process is followed, situations and outcomes can differ.

If the cruelty report is related to a puppy mill, a team effort is usually necessary, and it will likely include a veterinarian and a humane organization that is prepared to help seize and care for 200 or more dogs. If the dogs have been neglected, they will need immediate veterinary care, and some will have to be euthanized. The circumstances will be documented and evidence collected. One of the biggest challenges is housing 200 or more dogs, including sick dogs and puppies, while the legal process runs its course. Unless the breeder voluntarily relinquishes ownership, the dogs usually remain the property of the breeder until the final resolution of the trial or appeal. This means that the dogs cannot be spayed or neutered and that permanent homes cannot be found for them. Because of limited resources and the housing problem faced by smaller cities and towns, where many of these puppy mills are located, law enforcement may hesitate to investigate or seize dogs from a puppy mill without assistance from a humane organization.

Once the evidence is gathered, the prosecutor evaluates the case and decides whether or not to go forward with the prosecution. She will look at the sufficiency of the evidence, the seriousness of the offense, the city or county's available resources, any alternatives that may be available, the defendant's criminal record if any, and the court's caseload. A prosecutor or district attorney's commitment to prosecuting animal cruelty is extremely important. District attorneys have what is known as "prosecutorial discretion," which means they have the ultimate say on whether or not to proceed with a case. Unfortunately, there remains the belief among some district attorneys and law enforcement personnel that animal cruelty is not an important crime. Therefore, they may decline to prosecute cases, even if the evidence is strong.

Case in Point

In Van Zandt County, Texas, a bulldog was brutally choked and beaten with a hammer while tethered to a tree. The man who beat the dog admitted to killing the dog. The grand jury failed to support an indictment. What happened to this seemingly clear-cut case of animal cruelty? What evidence did the district attorney present that resulted in a "no bill" from the grand jury?

If a decision is made to go forward, the prosecuting attorney will decide whether to file felony or misdemeanor charges based on the facts and evidence gathered. There will be a trial or possibly a plea bargain. A defendant's lawyer may decide to try to negotiate a guilty plea in exchange for a lesser sentence for his client. If the prosecutor and the judge agree, the defendant does not have to go through a trial, and the case is over. If the case proceeds to trial, the defendant has the choice of whether to have a jury trial or a bench trial (with a judge). Animal cruelty trials have a tendency to generate a great deal of public emotion, and animal advocates often attend as a show of support for the district attorney's office and the animal. Significant media coverage surrounds animal cruelty cases, especially large seizures at puppy mills and particularly brutal abuse cases.

FOR OWNERS: Animal cruelty is serious. Whether negligent or intentional, dogs suffer at the hands of humans. Educate yourself. Know the law and what is required of you as a dog owner. Many cities have classes you can take on owning and caring for a dog. Do not hesitate to report animal cruelty if you see it.

FOR LAWYERS: Most lawyers will never find themselves in the position of defending or prosecuting a case of animal cruelty. However, certain crimes, such as animal cruelty, are of concern to everyone, particularly those in the legal system. Know your state's laws and enforcement record in animal cruelty, and work to strengthen those laws as well as their enforcement.

Chapter 6

WHEN YOUR DOG IS LEFT WITHOUT YOU

In the event of your disability or death, family and friends will step in to care for you or make the various arrangements that need to be made. To the extent that you plan ahead and make your wishes known, verbally and in writing, you make it easier for loved ones to fulfill those wishes when you die or experience a catastrophic illness. This is also true when it comes to the care of your dogs. Planning for the future should include making arrangements for the faithful companions with whom you share your life. It is an important step for everyone, whether you are young, have a large family, or know lots of animal lovers. Do not assume that someone will step in if you can no longer take care of your dog. Sadly, thousands of beloved animals are euthanized every year because their owners made assumptions and failed to plan ahead.

The good news is that more legal options are available than ever before for the long-term care of companion animals. New laws are being passed, courts are recognizing people's wishes, and "retirement homes" are being established that provide animals with loving homes and companionship.

Beyond the natural reluctance to plan for their own passing, people often make the mistake of assuming that plans for companion animals are not necessary—that family members or friends will take them and love them the way we do. It may not happen. Unfortunately, family members simply may be unable to take care of your dog. Even if they agreed in the past to help, or if they very much want to help, at the time of your death their circumstances may have changed. They may live in a pet-restricted environment or have reached the maximum number of animals allowed. They may have developed physical challenges that prevent them from caring for your dog, or they simply may be unable to do so financially. And if you have not made alternative plans, your friend or family member may believe the only option is to give your dog away or to take your dog to a shelter. It happens all too frequently.

Fortunately, with a little planning, you can ensure that your dog is provided for in the event of your death or disability.

Wills

Several legal avenues are available that will allow you to arrange for the care of your dog. All have pros and cons to consider. The most common is your last will and testament. A will, medical directive, and other related documents are extremely important, with or without companion animals. Regardless of your age or the size of your assets, legally setting out your wishes in the event of a catastrophic illness or death will lessen the burden on your family during a difficult time and will make clear your wishes regarding your health decisions.

A will becomes operative in the event of your death. It is one way in which you can provide for the future care of your dog, as well as arrange your funeral, pay remaining expenses, remember loved ones, and distribute your assets. There are some drawbacks with a will when arranging for the care of your dog, although most can be overcome with some additional planning. So if you do not have a will, drafting one is your first order of business.

The laws regarding wills and trusts are state-specific and can be complex, so it is important to seek the advice of a lawyer in drafting your will. Handwritten, or holographic, wills are legal in some states; but, if possible, do not depend on a handwritten will. A will is a document you want interpreted clearly.

There are generally no statutes or specific provisions regarding bequests of companion animals. Dogs are classified as personal property, so most laws that relate to the disposition of personal property will apply to your dog. Public policy regarding estate planning is that you are generally free to dispose of your property in any way you wish, within certain legal constraints. For example, a bequest will fail if it is criminal in nature. As for dogs, it is not advisable to designate in your will that your dog is to be euthanized when you die. Some owners have such strong bonds that they believe no one else can properly care for their dogs or that their dogs will endlessly grieve after their deaths. While it is true that we develop strong bonds with our dogs, they are quite resilient and can form new bonds. We have seen it time and again with rescue dogs, who go on to be placed in happy new forever homes. Once placed in a loving home, most dogs can develop trust again and live a happy life.

For wills that do include provisions that the decedent's animals be euthanized, whether or not the provision is carried out depends largely on the executor. Some executors seek to carry out the wishes of the testator and will find a veterinarian to euthanize the dog. However, if the executor is uncomfortable doing that or if there is a challenge to the will, a judge may find that euthanizing a healthy dog, particularly if there is a willing adopter, conflicts with public policy and may strike that instruction from the will.

Case in Point

In the case of *In Re Capers Estate*, Ida M. Capers directed in her will that her two Irish setters, Brickland and Sunny Birch, be "destroyed in a humane manner" at the time of her death.[1] The executors, uncomfortable with carrying out the provision, filed a petition with the court for

Continued

1. *In Re Capers Estate*, 34 Pa. D. & C.2d 121, 122 (Orphans' Ct. Allegheny Cnty. 1964).

Case in Point *Continued*

a declaratory judgment. The judge stated that it "would be unethical to carry out the literal provisions . . . of decedent's will. [It] would confiscate the life of two setters for no purpose. It would be an act of cruelty that is not sanctioned by the traditions and purposes of this court, and would conflict with its established public policy."[2]

The Gift of Your Dog

A bequest, or gift, of your dog in your will to a beneficiary transfers ownership from your estate to the person you designate. In order to use your will to provide for your dog, you must have a beneficiary, a person you know and trust, to whom you will give your dog. You need to know that this person will provide your dog with a good home. Because ownership is transferred from your estate to the beneficiary, there are no ongoing checks and balances, as in a trust agreement. You can request that your executor or someone else check on your dog, but there is no guarantee that it will happen. The purpose of a will is to distribute your assets and close your estate. If you use a will, you need to do your due diligence in advance to find the right person.

If a trusted family member or friend has agreed to take your dog upon your death, you can give that person your dog as a bequest in your will or have your lawyer draft a codicil if you already have a will. A codicil amends your will, allowing you to keep your existing will in place. Having the transfer of your dog in your will legally validates your wishes and eliminates questions as to what your intentions were regarding the future care of your dog. In addition to the bequest of your dog, it is advisable to leave a gift of cash or an asset of value to the beneficiary to assist with your dog's care. Even if the individual does not need the money, it is a way to show your appreciation for his or her commitment. Do not leave an exorbitant

2. *Id.* at 132.

amount, especially if it would leave your human heirs out in the cold, as it may raise the possibility of a challenge to your will. This is another reason why it is important to work with a lawyer—to ensure that your wishes are fulfilled while reducing the risk of a challenge. The language must be clear so that there is little question regarding your intent. Although no one can guarantee that there will not be a challenge, a lawyer can advise you of the risks and strengthen your position.

Case in Point

Florence B. Lyon designated in her will that $1.4 million be used for the care of her animals. In a challenge to the will, the court found that the language of the will appeared to create a trust, but it could not be given effect because she did not name a person to enforce the trust. The court also found that while Ms. Lyon's intent was to care for her animals, she was mistaken in the amount that would be necessary for that purpose. The court reduced the amount of the bequest but set out specific instructions for the care of her animals until their deaths.[3]

Do not leave your dog to someone in your will without that person's prior knowledge. Even if it is a family member or if the person has agreed verbally, make sure he knows that you are serious and plan to put it in your will. Discuss the obligations and responsibilities thoroughly. You are legally transferring ownership of your dog, so you want the person to think seriously about the commitment before agreeing to it. Never depend solely on a verbal agreement. Even with witnesses, you will not be around to explain your intent. If the person is sincere, she will agree to being included in a written will.

When drafting the provision in your will, consider any other circumstances under which the bequest will occur. Some testators have

3. *In re Lyon Estate*, 67 Pa. D. & C.2d 474 (Ct. Com. Pl. Franklin Cnty. 1974).

gone so far as to leave their homes to the beneficiary so the dogs will not have to leave their environment. Some bequests designate that the beneficiary is to take two dogs who have grown up together and should not be separated. So, while your bequest will transfer ownership to the person you've designated, you can attach certain circumstances. A lawyer can assist you in determining what restrictions are valid and enforceable under your state's laws.

Situations change and bequests can be refused, so be sure to designate at least one alternative person in the event that the original individual who has agreed to care for your dog is unable or unwilling to accept that responsibility. Periodically review the arrangements you have made for your dog in the same way you review your other estate-planning issues.

Nothing is foolproof, and one drawback with a will bequest is that it is effective only upon your death. If you become disabled and cannot care for your dog, you have to make other arrangements. One option is a pet trust, which is explained later in this chapter. The other drawback to a will is the time lag between your passing and the probate of the will. You must arrange for the immediate care of your dog until the will is probated or during a challenge to the will. You can discuss temporary arrangements with your executor, the beneficiary, and/or your lawyer.

When drafting a will, do not leave a gift of money or any other asset directly to your dog. Your dog is personal property, and you cannot leave money to personal property. Any cash or assets must be given to your dog's caretaker or another human for the care of your dog.

Case in Point

Ms. Eliza R. Thompson bequeathed $50 to $100 a year to her two dogs, Fox and Rover, for as long as they would live.[4] Ms. Thompson's bequests to Fox and Rover were not valid.

4. Greenwood v. Henry et al., 52 N.J. Eq. 447 (Ch. Ct. N.J. 1894).

Alternatives to a Will

If you do not have a family member or friend willing to take your dog, you can consider an arrangement with a shelter, rescue group, or humane organization. A donation may provide the organization with the ability to care for your dog on a short-term basis while trying to adopt your dog. Many of the larger humane organizations have planned-giving directors or outside lawyers who can advise you. There is no guarantee. Very few of these organizations, even larger ones, have facilities that allow them to keep dogs on a long-term basis. The smaller ones work on a shoestring budget and may not have the resources when the time comes to take your dog. The larger ones will provide a bit more security, but if your dog is older, has health issues, or has problems with aggression, she will not be at the top of the adoption list. This option may provide you only with the assurance that a potential adopter will be carefully vetted or that your dog will be humanely euthanized if not adopted.

Another option is to find a "retirement home" for the care of your dog. There are a few homes around the country that have been established with the specific purpose of caring for companion animals in the event that an owner requires an extended hospital stay, moves to a retirement home, or predeceases an animal. Retirement homes for dogs have not entered the mainstream and they are usually expensive. However, if you have the funds, it is one way to ensure that your dog is well cared for in a homelike environment for the remainder of his life.

Case in Point

The Stevenson Companion Animal Life-Care Center was established by the Texas A&M College of Veterinary Medicine. It "provides the physical, emotional, and medical needs of companion animals whose owners are no longer able to provide that care."[5]

5. To learn more about the Texas A&M Stevenson Companion Animal Life-Care Center, *see* https://vetmed.tamu.edu/stevenson-center/about (last visited May 9, 2014).

FOR LAWYERS: Leaving money for the care of a pet is still relatively new and can be controversial, particularly with those heirs who are in line to inherit. Make sure you know the law and have read the case law in your state, and even in other states, regarding challenges. Talk with lawyers who have experience in these matters. The language in the bequest should be clear. Determine an amount of money that is realistic for the care of the dog until she dies. Heirs may complain, and the courts may strike provisions they consider unreasonable for the care of a dog.

FOR OWNERS: In using a will to plan for the care of your dog, the most important decision is selecting someone you trust who will agree to care for your dog. A will does not provide for the ongoing supervision of the care your dog receives. Also, plan for the time between your death and the time your will is probated or in the event of a challenge to your will.

Pet Trusts

Another option to consider in planning for the care of your dog is a pet trust. A trust is more complicated than a will, but it includes oversight, along with checks and balances, and it can be used in the event of a disability in addition to death. A trust for the care of a companion animal is nothing new, but in the past they were called honorary trusts, without the force of statutory law behind them. An honorary trust is set up with the hope that the person can, and will, fulfill the provisions of the trust. It has various legal problems, not the least of which is its potential lack of enforceability. There is no designated human who can legally enforce the provisions of the trust. Also, honorary trusts may violate the Rule Against Perpetuities, an historical rule from England that is still in effect in some states, which requires a future interest in property to vest within a set period of time. Although legally problematic, honorary trusts have been the only options for people who wanted to set up a trust for the care of their pets. And some courts have validated them but statutory pet trusts are the best option.

Today, honorary trusts remain the only trust option for residents of the few remaining states that have failed to pass pet trust legislation. Fortunately, the majority of states have passed pet trust laws, and others will likely follow. This trend is a major development in animal law and is a positive advancement of the position of animals in society. State pet trusts are usually based on the Trust for Care of Animal, a model law in the Uniform Trust Code that was drafted by the National Conference of Commissioners on Uniform State Laws. Unlike regular trusts that designate a trustee, a settlor (or grantor), and a beneficiary, pet trusts have a trustee, a settlor (or grantor), a beneficiary (the animal), *and* a caretaker, the person who receives the funds and is responsible for the day-to-day care and well-being of the animal.

Case in Point

The Trust for Care of Animal states:

> (a) A trust may be created to provide for the care of an animal alive during the settlor's lifetime. The trust terminates upon the death of the animal or, if the trust was created to provide for the care of more than one animal alive during the settlor's lifetime, upon the death of the last surviving animal.
> (b) A trust authorized by this section may be enforced by a person appointed in the terms of the trust or, if no person is so appointed, by a person appointed by the court. A person having an interest in the welfare of the animal may request the court to appoint a person to enforce the trust or to remove a person appointed.
> (c) Property of a trust authorized by this section may be applied only to its intended use, except to the extent the court determines that the value of the trust property exceeds the amount required for the intended use. Except as otherwise provided in the terms of the trust, property not required for the intended use must be distributed to the settlor, if then living, otherwise to the settlor's successors in interest.[6]

6. UNIFORM TRUST CODE, http://www.uniformlaws.org/shared/docs/trust_code/utc_final_rev2010.pdf, at 65-67 (last visited Sept. 6, 2014).

Statutory pet trusts address the legal problems of honorary trusts, are enforceable in a court of law, and do not rely solely on the good intentions of the parties. All states should have them and probably will at some point in the future. Statutory pet trusts address the Rule Against Perpetuities by ending the trust upon the death of the last surviving animal or at some other set time. The trust establishes a method of enforcement through the language in section (b) above. The above law is a model that some states have used verbatim, while other states have adapted their own language.

Case in Point

Oklahoma's Validity of a Trust for the Care of Domestic or Pet Animals

...

B. The instrument creating the trust shall be liberally construed . . . to presume against the mere precatory or honorary nature of the disposition, and to carry out the general intent of the transferor.

C. . . . The trustee of a trust created in accordance with this section shall ensure that care is provided for the benefit of the animal in accordance with the terms of the trust or, in absence of any terms, shall ensure that care is provided that is reasonable under the circumstances. The trustee may employ agents or contractors to provide any care and pay for the care from the assets of the trust. The trustee shall also ensure that the property of a trust authorized by this section is applied only to its intended use.

D. A trust authorized by this section may be enforced by a person appointed in the trust instrument, the caretaker of the designated animal or animals, and the remainder beneficiary, or, if none, by an individual appointed by a court upon application to it by an individual.[7]

As you can see in Oklahoma's law, the provisions ensure that the intent of the trust is followed; validate the trust, making it distinct from an honorary trust; allow the trustee flexibility in expenditures regarding care of the animal; and designate enforcement of the trust.

7. 60 OKLA. STAT. ANN. § 199 (2014).

If you want to set up a pet trust, you first need to know whether they are legal in your state. A lawyer should draft the trust, and he or she can confirm whether your trust would be an honorary trust or a pet trust under your state's trust law. A trust can be a testamentary trust, which is part of your will and takes effect upon your death, or an inter vivos, or living, trust, which can take effect during your lifetime if you become disabled.

In setting up a trust, you must do the following:

- Determine the caretaker. This person is very important, as this is the person who will be responsible for the day-to-day care of your dog. Choose someone you trust; and that individual must know what is involved and agree to be the caretaker.

Case in Point

Remember Leona Helmsley's dog Trouble? She designated her brother as Trouble's caretaker and he reportedly didn't want Trouble.

- Designate a trustee. This person will manage the funds to be used for the care of your dog. *The trustee and caretaker should never be the same person.* The only situation in which you have true checks and balances is when the caretaker and trustee are two different people.
- Make sure the trust document applies to any animals living at the time of your death or disability. If the trust covers only Spot and now you have Spot and Lucy, you will have to change the trust.
- Determine the money and other assets that will make up the trust. This will depend on your financial situation, the number of dogs you have, and any special needs your dogs have that require special or ongoing veterinary care. A lawyer experienced in drafting pet trusts can assist you in determining how much money should be in the trust. Some pet trust statutes include a provision that allows a judge to change the amount if it is deemed unreasonable by the court.

Case in Point

Bringing up Leona Helmsley again, she left Trouble $12 million, which the court reduced to $2 million, still a great deal of money for the care of a small dog.

- It is also advisable to include payment to the caretaker for her services but at the same time to ensure that the trustee will monitor the caretaker's services.

Case in Point

There are cases in which caretakers have fraudulently "extended" the life of a dog by many years beyond the norm in order to continue to receive payments. In these schemes, the caretaker buys a new dog to replace the original dog when she dies. Make sure the caretaker cannot give your dog or cat nine lives.

- Identify your dog. If your dog has not been microchipped, have it done. Set up a file on each dog, with a picture, and include such information as her age, any health issues, her veterinarian, her food, and specific needs. Is your dog good with children? Other dogs? Cats?
- Define the care your dog is to receive. Your instructions can be as detailed as you wish. Instructions such as how often to take him to the veterinarian, the amount of exercise he needs, and where he sleeps are important. This is one advantage of a trust document—the ability to set out the specifics of how the trust funds will be spent and the care your dog is to receive.
- Specify under what circumstances it is acceptable to euthanize your dog. Some owners want certification from two veterinarians that the dog's condition is terminal and that euthanasia is in the best interest of the dog. Some owners will leave it to the discretion of the caretaker. It is your decision.

- Designate where the money is to go when your animals die if funds remain in the trust. You can designate a charitable organization or family. Just make sure you include it. Many pet trusts have default provisions giving the remainder to the heirs if no designation is made.
- If you set up an inter vivos, or living, trust you may be required to fund it immediately. A lawyer can advise you of the laws in your state. Additionally, you can choose to fully fund it upon your death with assets from your estate.

As you can see, trusts are more complicated than wills, but they provide more flexibility and control. A lawyer can walk you through the myriad rules and cases that apply and assist you in making the best decision for your dog.

In an Emergency

What would happen if you were in an accident and could not get home to take care of your dog? It could happen, so it is important to have a plan in place in the event of a sudden emergency. Some owners post signs on their doors or windows indicating that they have animals in the house in the event of a fire. It is also a good idea to carry a card along with your driver's license, indicating that you have animals at home and who should be contacted in the event of an accident.

You can have agreements with your neighbors, friends, or family to take care of your dog in the event of an emergency. Neighbors are usually more than happy to agree to help in an emergency situation, but they need to know what to do. Always have more than one person on call, and they should be people you know personally. You don't want to spend six weeks in the hospital only to find out that your neighbor was on vacation and unaware of the circumstances.

Natural Disasters

No one can really be prepared for a disaster. Hurricanes, tornadoes, and wildfires can cause widespread destruction and loss of lives. Hurricane

Katrina in New Orleans was one such disaster, and it taught the country some hard lessons about saving people and animals.

The evacuation of the citizens of New Orleans included no procedures for rescuing companion animals, and many people were forced to leave their homes without their beloved dogs. Beyond the human tragedy, heartbreaking images were shown of dogs stranded on rooftops, running after cars that carried their humans, and wandering the empty streets of New Orleans looking for food.

In order to prevent another Katrina disaster for companion animals, Congress passed the Pets Evacuation and Transportation Standards Act of 2006. It requires a city or state receiving federal funds to include how it will address the needs of individuals with household pets and service animals in the event of a disaster. Know your state's laws regarding the procedures required in the event of an emergency.

Conclusion

It is said that knowledge is power.[1] With that in mind, I hope that the knowledge you have gleaned from this book has given you the best kind of power—to resolve conflicts, understand the law, and protect the dogs who love us unconditionally. Beyond knowledge, I hope that you have greater insight and appreciation into the work that is behind all of the laws in place that have assimilated our dogs into our everyday lives.

If you are active in animal protection, I hope the book has enhanced your knowledge in some way that supports the work you do. For those of you who have been on the sidelines, perhaps something in this book has inspired you and given you ideas on how to take an active role in speaking for those who have no voice. Participation can be as simple and important as a two-minute call to your legislator.

Many of the laws I have covered in this book are part of a larger, ongoing public policy dialogue about what our relationship should be with companion animals and with animals in general. Every aspect of our relationship is being questioned—from ownership to valuation to the retail sales of animals. And rightly so. At no other time in our history have companion animals played such a large and important role in our lives.

1. An expression attributed to Francis Bacon, a 17th-century philosopher, author, and lawyer.

Appendix

TERMS AND DEFINITIONS

Adoption: Rescue groups and shelters usually use the word "adoption" rather than "sale" to refer to the transfer of ownership of animals in their agreements.

Bailment: A situation in which one person accepts property from another for a certain purpose, such as a dog groomer taking temporary possession of a dog for the purpose of grooming. Ownership of the property does not change, and the property is returned to the owner.

Bills: Proposed laws that are introduced by senators and representatives at state and federal levels.

Case law: Body of law comprised of cases that have been decided judicially and become legal precedent.

Cause of action: Facts and the legal theory that form the basis of, and justify, a lawsuit.

Citizen suit provision: A provision in a law that allows a private citizen to file a lawsuit to enforce a statute.

Civil law: Area of the law covering disputes between individuals, organizations, or companies involving private rights and monetary compensation. Also, the legal system followed by Louisiana based on the French civil system of law.

Common law: Body of law in the United States that has been established through judicial decisions.

Companion animal: A term that is replacing the word "pet" and that is considered to be more accurate in its description of our relationship with dogs.

Criminal law: Body of law involving crimes against the state and its citizens. Punishment may involve jail time.

Crush videos: Videos in which women crush small animals, including dogs, with their bare feet or in stiletto heels to satisfy the viewer's sexual fetish.

Damages: Money claimed as compensation for loss or injury in a lawsuit.

Exemplary damages: Punitive damages.

Federal Register: A publication where federal regulations, and proposed regulations, are published.

Felony: A serious crime that typically involves jail time.

Jurisdiction: A court's power to hear a case based on, for example, a geographic area or a statute.

Legislation: Laws or set of laws enacted by a government.

Misdemeanor: A minor crime.

Ordinance: A law enacted by a city or town.

Personal property: Property that is not real property or intellectual property. Dogs are personal property.

Police power: The authority of the state to make laws and pass regulations in order to protect its citizens.

Precedent: A court opinion that is the basis for deciding future, similar cases.

Puppy mill: A large-scale commercial breeding operation whose motivation is pure profit, with little or no concern for animal welfare except as it benefits the business.

Rescue group: A group, usually a nonprofit, whose sole mission is to find homes for abandoned or relinquished animals.

Right to due process: A citizen's constitutional right to legal proceedings that are fair and established.

Rules and regulations: Statutes that become laws may be broad mandates and are interpreted and published through rules and regulations.

Service animals: Under the Americans with Disabilities Act, service animals are defined as dogs that are individually trained to do work or perform tasks for people with disabilities.

Shelter: A municipal entity that takes animals who are relinquished and is charged with overseeing their adoption, turning them over to a rescue group, or euthanizing them.

Statute: A bill that is passed by a legislature and becomes law.

Statute of limitations: A time limit, after which a person cannot legally file a lawsuit.

Therapy dogs: Dogs trained to provide comfort to people, for example, in hospitals and nursing homes.

Acronyms

ACAA: Air Carriers Access Act
ADA: Americans with Disabilities Act
APHIS: Animal and Plant Health Inspection Service
AVMA: American Veterinary Medical Association
AWA: Animal Welfare Act
CFR: Code of Federal Regulations
FHA: Fair Housing Act
FPLA: Fur Products Labeling Act
HUD: Housing and Urban Development
NIBRS: National Incident-Based Reporting System
OIG: Office of the Inspector General
PETS: Pets Evacuation and Transportation Standards Act of 2006
PTO: Patent and Trademark Office
SLAPPs: Strategic lawsuits against public participation
USDA: United States Department of Agriculture

Index